SAUDI ARABIA'S TROUBLING EDUCATIONAL CURRICULUM

HEARING

BEFORE THE

SUBCOMMITTEE ON TERRORISM, NONPROLIFERATION, AND TRADE

OF THE

COMMITTEE ON FOREIGN AFFAIRS
HOUSE OF REPRESENTATIVES

ONE HUNDRED FIFTEENTH CONGRESS

FIRST SESSION

JULY 19, 2017

Serial No. 115–46

Printed for the use of the Committee on Foreign Affairs

Available via the World Wide Web: http://www.foreignaffairs.house.gov/ or
http://www.gpo.gov/fdsys/

U.S. GOVERNMENT PUBLISHING OFFICE

26–312PDF   WASHINGTON : 2017

For sale by the Superintendent of Documents, U.S. Government Publishing Office
Internet: bookstore.gpo.gov Phone: toll free (866) 512–1800; DC area (202) 512–1800
Fax: (202) 512–2104 Mail: Stop IDCC, Washington, DC 20402–0001

COMMITTEE ON FOREIGN AFFAIRS

EDWARD R. ROYCE, California, *Chairman*

CHRISTOPHER H. SMITH, New Jersey
ILEANA ROS-LEHTINEN, Florida
DANA ROHRABACHER, California
STEVE CHABOT, Ohio
JOE WILSON, South Carolina
MICHAEL T. McCAUL, Texas
TED POE, Texas
DARRELL E. ISSA, California
TOM MARINO, Pennsylvania
JEFF DUNCAN, South Carolina
MO BROOKS, Alabama
PAUL COOK, California
SCOTT PERRY, Pennsylvania
RON DeSANTIS, Florida
MARK MEADOWS, North Carolina
TED S. YOHO, Florida
ADAM KINZINGER, Illinois
LEE M. ZELDIN, New York
DANIEL M. DONOVAN, Jr., New York
F. JAMES SENSENBRENNER, Jr.,
  Wisconsin
ANN WAGNER, Missouri
BRIAN J. MAST, Florida
FRANCIS ROONEY, Florida
BRIAN K. FITZPATRICK, Pennsylvania
THOMAS A. GARRETT, Jr., Virginia

ELIOT L. ENGEL, New York
BRAD SHERMAN, California
GREGORY W. MEEKS, New York
ALBIO SIRES, New Jersey
GERALD E. CONNOLLY, Virginia
THEODORE E. DEUTCH, Florida
KAREN BASS, California
WILLIAM R. KEATING, Massachusetts
DAVID N. CICILLINE, Rhode Island
AMI BERA, California
LOIS FRANKEL, Florida
TULSI GABBARD, Hawaii
JOAQUIN CASTRO, Texas
ROBIN L. KELLY, Illinois
BRENDAN F. BOYLE, Pennsylvania
DINA TITUS, Nevada
NORMA J. TORRES, California
BRADLEY SCOTT SCHNEIDER, Illinois
THOMAS R. SUOZZI, New York
ADRIANO ESPAILLAT, New York
TED LIEU, California

AMY PORTER, *Chief of Staff*   THOMAS SHEEHY, *Staff Director*
JASON STEINBAUM, *Democratic Staff Director*

SUBCOMMITTEE ON TERRORISM, NONPROLIFERATION, AND TRADE

TED POE, Texas, *Chairman*

JOE WILSON, South Carolina
DARRELL E. ISSA, California
PAUL COOK, California
SCOTT PERRY, Pennsylvania
LEE M. ZELDIN, New York
BRIAN J. MAST, Florida
THOMAS A. GARRETT, Jr., Virginia

WILLIAM R. KEATING, Massachusetts
LOIS FRANKEL, Florida
BRENDAN F. BOYLE, Pennsylvania
DINA TITUS, Nevada
NORMA J. TORRES, California
BRADLEY SCOTT SCHNEIDER, Illinois

CONTENTS

Page

SAUDI ARABIA'S TROUBLING EDUCATIONAL CURRICULUM

WEDNESDAY, JULY 19, 2017

House of Representatives,
Subcommittee on Terrorism, Nonproliferation, and Trade,
Committee on Foreign Affairs,
Washington, DC.

The subcommittee met, pursuant to notice, at 2:15 p.m., in room 2200 Rayburn House Office Building, Hon. Ted Poe (chairman of the subcommittee) presiding.

Mr. POE. The subcommittee will now come to order.

Without objection, all members may have 5 days to submit statements, questions, and extraneous materials for the record, subject to the limitation in the rules.

The Chair will ask that the witnesses come forward and sit in your designated positions.

The Chair has distributed to all members an expert from—excerpts from current textbooks published by Saudi Arabia's Ministry of Education. The Chair would ask and direct that the staff furnish this material to all of the witnesses at this time.

Saudi Arabia is an ally in the fight against terrorism. Many of the same terrorist organizations that threaten the United States also desire to overthrow the Saudi Government and break our partnership with the government. It is a key member of the Coalition to Fight ISIS, with its pilots flying alongside Americans since day one of the campaign in Syria. Last year Saudi Arabia adopted strict laws prohibiting fundraising for terrorism, jointly designated support networks for al-Qaeda and the Taliban.

However, the Saudis still have much more they need to do at home to counter the sources of extremism in the region. The battle against terrorism will ultimately have to be fought and won on the battlefield of ideas. Saudi Arabia has simply not done enough to defeat extremist ideology.

The Kingdom is playing the role of both arsonist and firefighter when it comes to Islamic extremism. Nowhere is this more evident than the textbooks Saudi Arabia produces to teach young people. For too long, Saudi Arabia's education curriculum has inspired the very ideology that is at the root of many terrorist organizations like ISIS and al-Qaeda. Saudi textbooks are full of anti-Semitism, conspiracy theories, and calls to violence that have incited students both at home and across the world.

This poisonous ideology has provided the groundwork for generations of extremism. In fact, ISIS adopted official Saudi textbooks

(1)

for its schools in 2015 until that terrorist organization could publish its own textbooks. However, its export of hateful material through Saudi-funded schools abroad has helped spread the toxic ideology to more tolerant and open Muslim communities in countries such as Kosovo and Indonesia.

While the Kingdom has repeatedly pledged to remove extremist content from its curriculum, troubling language remains in many of the most recent editions of Saudi textbooks. In 2006, the Saudis committed to eliminate all passages that promoted hatred toward any religion by 2008. Yet even today, years later, textbooks include content that discourages befriending infidels, claims the goal of Zionism is world domination, and encourages fighting any infidel who refuses to submit to the supremacy of Islam. This intolerance is unacceptable and directly contributes to the widespread persecution of religious minorities that plague the Middle East.

Another passage in a current Saudi textbook for middle school students states that "the mujahideen who are doing good deeds for the sake of Allah . . . should be given transportation, weapons, food, and anything else that they may need to continue their jihad." Messages such as this undermine the Saudi's own counterterrorism efforts. By indoctrinating children into the belief that the people of other faiths are inferior or that are a threat to Islam, Saudi Arabia is ensuring future generations of extremists that will join the ranks of terrorist groups.

This is not to ignore that some positive steps have been taken. In recent years, the Kingdom has introduced passages that denounce terrorism and encourage dialogue with other faiths. But these steps only send mixed messages to easily influenced young minds so as long as those more extreme messages remain.

The State Department has previously in other administrations, failed to hold Saudi Arabia counterparts to past pledges. The Saudi—the State Department has even refused to publish reports that shed light on these troubling textbooks for fear of embarrassing our Saudi partners, information that they have in the possession of the State Department. This is troubling.

While we appreciate Saudi Arabia's contribution to our overall counterterrorism efforts in the region, we must hold them accountable for their role in fueling the very extremism that we are both trying to combat. It is in both of our countries' interests in the fight against terrorism. We all need to be on the same page. And that is just the way it is.

I will yield from the gentleman from Massachusetts Mr. Keating, the ranking member, for his opening statement.

Mr. KEATING. Thank you, Chairman Poe, for holding this hearing. And thank you to our witnesses for being here. Mr. Wolf, welcome back.

We have dedicated a lot of time in this subcommittee with talks of countering terrorism and violent extremism. Our last hearing addressed that very issue in Europe, in light of the many attacks carried out against so many innocent civilians across the region.

We are here to discuss the issue in the context of Saudi Arabia's school curriculum, and in particular, reforms that have been made to ensure children just going to school are not being trained in intolerance and violence but, also importantly, to identify what work still must be done. The spread of extremist ideologies and instances of individuals being inspired to commit acts of terrorism has forced us to learn much, much more about the factors that make individuals vulnerable to committing acts of violence and taking human lives.

We realize that the messages these individuals are exposed to can change the course of their lives and push them to carry out heinous crimes of their own in their own communities, and in those communities they may have never known, but their actions have led to dehumanization, and they actually come to believe legitimate targets of violence are their victims.

These materials that our future generations spend every day of the most formative years of their lives learning from are therefore very important. Texts that dehumanize and condone violence against others simply cannot be tolerated.

Saudi Arabia is an ally of the United States in fighting terrorism. And if there is ever to be a lasting peace and security in the Middle East it will require every country in the region stepping up and being a leader in eradicating extremism and promoting the institutions and rule of law needed to ensure that such hatred and violent ideologies are never again permitted to take root or to spread.

Today I hope to learn more from our witnesses about the reforms and progress the Kingdom has already made, what existing challenges lie before us and, specifically, how we in Congress can support progress in this regard. Every year that goes by children are being taught intolerance. And that compounds the challenges we will face in creating a safer world for them to grow up in going forward.

So, I am looking forward to today's hearing about the steps that can be made sure to take these materials molding our future generations and bringing them forward, not only in Saudi Arabia but in communities around the world. We all have forms of intolerance, and we all must work to remove these from our own countries. This must be achieved as quickly as possible, however. We cannot afford to be patient while intolerance that promotes or condones violence in any form is not only shared but taught and continues to undermine our collective efforts to protect communities from terrorism and violent extremism.

Again I would like to thank our witnesses and I yield back.

Mr. POE. I thank the gentleman from Massachusetts.

Do any other members wish to be recognized?

[No response.]

Mr. POE. Seeing none, without objection all witnesses' prepared statements will be made part of the record. I ask that each witness please keep your presentation to no more than 5 minutes. If you see a red light that appears before you, that means stop. And we do have your statements and all members have had access to those statements for some time.

I will introduce each witness and then give them time for their opening statements.

Ms. Nina Shea is the director of the Center for Religious Freedom at the Hudson Institute. Previously she was appointed by the United States House of Representatives to serve seven terms as a commissioner on the U.S. Commission on International Religious Freedom.

Dr. David Weinberg is a senior fellow at the Foundation for Defense of Democracies. Prior to joining the FDD, he served as Democratic professional staff member at the House Committee on Foreign Affairs.

The Honorable Frank Wolf served, God bless you, 17 terms in the United States House of Representatives. He is now a distinguished senior fellow at the 21st Century Wilberforce Initiative.

And Dr. Douglas Johnston is the president emeritus and founder of the International Center for Religion and Diplomacy. Prior to his current position he served as vice president and COO of Center for Strategic and International Studies.

Ms. Shea, we will start with you. You have 5 minutes.

STATEMENT OF MS. NINA SHEA, DIRECTOR, CENTER FOR RELIGIOUS FREEDOM, HUDSON INSTITUTE

Ms. SHEA. Thank you, Mr. Chairman and members of the committee.

This is an important hearing. It comes at a critical time when Saudi Arabia itself is expressing a new vision for itself of reform. And many thoughtful voices after 9/11 made a connection between the fact that most of the perpetrators and the mastermind behind those attacks were from Saudi Arabia, and that their educational system could have a lot to do with what happened that day.

The Saudis—the Saudi King—back in 2003 convened his own panel to examine the Saudi textbooks and they confirmed some of our worst fears. And they found that the Saudi Kingdom, and I am quoting, "religious studies curriculum encourages violence with others and misguides the people into believing that in order to safeguard their own religion they must violently repress and even physically eliminate the others."

For 15 years after 9/11 Saudi Ministry of Education textbooks still teach an ideology of hatred and violence against Jews, Christians, other Muslims such as Shiites, Sufis and Amadiyyas, Hindus, Baha'is, Yezidis, animists, sorcerers, and infidels of all stripes, as well as other groups with different beliefs. The most objectionable passages are from the upper grades' religious textbooks.

While the Saudi Government has made much of reform in the early grades, those religious texts, like those for math or English, have not been particularly problematic, though overall critical thinking and ideas that conflict with the government-approved ones are banned.

Each academic year the Ministry of Education issues a new edition of grades 1 through 12's religious textbooks. And they are mandatory in all Saudi public schools. Each edition reflects some changes in wording, content, and placement. Nevertheless, over the past some 10 years, the content, that I have been looking at these books, the content has continued to retain violent passages and directives.

Christians, Hindus, and those practicing witchcraft are to be fought and killed. The textbooks incite violence against polytheists, a category that would of course include all non-monotheistic religions, but in Saudi Wahhabi teaching can include monotheistic religions too, such as Christianity. Christians are also considered infidels who must be fought unless they have a protection contract with Muslims. Conspiracy theories are taught as fact about the Freemasons, the Rotary Club, the Lion's Club, the American University of Beirut, and so on.

Dogmatic lessons in Saudi middle and high school textbooks include that many—instruct that many Muslims should be killed for their beliefs, including blasphemers, Christian converts, and those who merely doubt the Prophet's truth, as well as Shiites and Sufis, who are condemned as polytheists for praying or even seen crying at gravesites.

No group, however, is more vilified than the Jews. The problem is far deeper than that conveyed by the State Department's characterization of it as simply stereotypical or anti-Semitic language. Repeatedly Jews are demonized, dehumanized, and targeted for violence. The textbooks instruct that the Zionist aim is Jewish domination of the world and controlling its destiny.

When I was in Saudi Arabia in 2011 with the U.S. Commission on International Religious Freedom I had a chance to ask the Saudi justice minister at the time why the Protocols of the Elders of Zion, an infamously anti-Semitic fabrication from the Russian revolution, is included in the textbooks on Hadith, which is the traditions of Islam's Prophet Mohammed, where it continues to be taught as historical fact. He responded that the Protocols are treated as part of Islamic culture because it is a book that has long been found in plentiful supply in Saudi Arabia and that it was a book that his father had in his house.

In the interests of time I am going to refer to my written testimony for specific examples. You have already cited a few.

But just to say that apostates are singled out for punishment in this life, death unless they repent within 3 days.

Christians, again, are considered polytheists, and polytheists are to be—is a reason to fight those who practice it and to commit jihad against it, is another quote from these books.

Homosexuals, the punishment is death.

Jihad is extolled and defined. Its first definition is asserting effort in fighting unbelievers and tyrants.

And there are many more examples. And these are posted on the Internet and shipped worldwide. And they have been linked by our counterterrorism officials to growing extremism.

The Saudis, the one point I would like to make is that the Saudis themselves have admitted that the textbooks need reform. They do not deny it. Any Saudi that I talked to has agreed, including the Saudi Minister of Education in 2011, but they have not really finished it. They have never finished it. And they have a long history of broken promises where they have said that they did; either they did clean them up, as our Ambassador to Washington, former Ambassador Turki al-Faisal told us, or that the reform is just around the corner and that it will be completed in 2 years or 5 years or 10 years. And over this period it has not happened.

The government—U.S. Government—has failed to verify this. And has even, as you mentioned, covered it up.

So, I will conclude my testimony there and urge you to mandate that Congress, mandate—that Congress mandate the State Department review the textbooks and highlight and detail the trouble-some portions of it. And to, even to make defense contracts with Saudi Arabia contingent on the cleanup of these textbooks and so that they are not in danger of hurting or killing any American that might be a member of the groups that are singled out for violence and dehumanization in these reports.

Thank you.

[The prepared statement of Ms. Shea follows:]

TESTIMONY OF NINA SHEA, DIRECTOR

HUDSON INSTITUTE'S CENTER FOR RELIGIOUS FREEDOM

BEFORE THE

HOUSE COMMITTEE ON FOREIGN AFFAIRS

"Saudi Arabia's Troubling Educational Curriculum"

July 19, 2017

Mr. Chairman, representing Hudson Institute's Center for Religious Freedom, I thank you for holding this important hearing today. It comes at an important time in the strengthening of United States and Saudi Arabia relations and when a new vision for Saudi Arabia by its rulers is being presented. In confronting Islamist extremist terror, we have a new opportunity to make a difference by examining the ideology reflected in Saudi Arabia's official textbooks.

After 9/11, when it became clear that 79 percent of the terrorists who waged the murderous attacks on American soil that day, not to mention the plot's mastermind, Osama bin Laden, were sons of Saudi Arabia, Saudi Arabia's education system was brought into question. The 9/11 Commission and other thoughtful voices suggested that the kingdom's interpretation of Islam, Wahhabism, which is taught as the core of its schools' standardized curriculum, could bear some responsibility for inciting violence against the West.

Soon after, with the help of Saudi-American journalist Ali Ahmed and several other American Muslims, who wish to remain anonymous, I began collecting, translating and analyzing Saudi textbooks for grades 1 through 12 of the Saudi religious curriculum. I published my findings in 2005, 2006, 2008 and 2011. In 2011, as a Commissioner on the U.S. Commission on International Religious Freedom, I visited Saudi Arabia and discussed its textbooks directly with the Minister of Education, the Minister of Justice and the Minister of Islamic Affairs. In subsequent years, I have studied and written about the global spread of Saudi Wahhabi education, including here in the academy operated by the Saudi embassy under the name Islamic Saudi Academy (for the academic year just concluded, its name was changed to King Abdullah Academy). My findings were generally validated by later reporting by the State Department and others.

The Saudi Textbooks

Fears that the Saudi government was indoctrinating its young people in violent and belligerent teachings toward us proved warranted. In 2003, a scholarly panel commissioned by Saudi King Abdullah reviewed the middle and high school religious curriculum for three subjects pertaining to Wahhabi Islam – Fiqh (law), Hadith (tradition), and Tawhid (beliefs regarding monotheism). Their conclusion was as shocking as it was blunt. At the 2003 National Dialogue in Saudi Arabia, these Saudi scholars presented their key finding that:

> [The Saudi Kingdom's religious studies curriculum] encourages violence towards others, and misguides the pupils into believing that in order to safeguard their own religion, they must violently repress and even physically eliminate the 'other.'

Sixteen years after 9/11, Saudi Ministry of Education textbooks still teach an ideology of hatred and violence against Jews, Christians, Muslims, such as Shiites, Sufis and Ahmadis, Hindus, Bahais, Yizidis, animists, sorcerers, and "infidels" of all stripes, as well as other groups with different beliefs. The most objectionable passages are found in the upper grades' religious textbooks. While the Saudi government has heralded reform for the early grades, those religious texts, like those for math and English, have not been particularly problematic, though, overall, critical thinking and ideas that conflict with the government approved ones are banned. (A Wahhabi educational document I analyzed had denounced "freedom of thinking" since it "let[s] loose the ideas and pens to write of disbelief as one likes, and put[s] ornaments on sin as one likes.")

Each academic year, Saudi Arabia's Ministry of Education publishes new editions of grades 1 through 12 religious textbooks, which are mandatory in the Saudi public schools. Each edition reflects some changes in wording, content and placement. Nevertheless, over the past some ten years, the content has continued to retain violent passages and directives.

Christians, Hindus and those "practicing witchcraft" are to be fought and killed. The textbooks incite violence against "polytheists," a category that would of course include all non-monotheistic religions but, in Saudi Wahhabi teaching, can include monotheistic religions, too. While Christianity is considered one of the three great monotheistic religions by the rest of the world, the Saudi textbooks teach that Christians are polytheists for their belief in Jesus Christ. Christians are also considered "infidels" who must be fought unless they have a protection contract with Muslims. Conspiracy theories are taught as fact about the Free Masons, the Rotary Club, the Lions Club and the American University of Beirut.

Dogmatic lessons in Saudi middle and high school textbooks instruct that many Muslims should be killed for their beliefs, including blasphemers, Christian converts, and those who merely "doubt" the Prophet's truth, as well as Shiites and Sufis, who are condemned as "polytheists" for praying or even seen crying at gravesites.

No group, however, is more vilified than Jews. The problem is far deeper than that conveyed by the State Department characterization of it as simply "stereotypical" or "anti-Semitic" language. Repeatedly, Jews are demonized, dehumanized, and targeted for violence. The textbooks instruct that the Zionist aim is "Jewish domination of the world and controlling its destiny." Israel's existence is de-legitimized and students are mentally prepared for eventual war with the Jews. All of Israel is called "occupied Islamic territory" (as are Romania, Bulgaria, Greece, much of Spain and the Balkans.)

When I met in 2011 with the then-Saudi justice minister Muhammad al-Issa, I asked him why the *Protocols of the Elders of Zion*, an infamously anti-Semitic fabrication from the Russian revolution period, is included in the textbook on Hadiths (traditions of Islam's Prophet Mohammed) where it continues to be taught as historical fact. He responded that the *Protocols* is treated as part of Islamic culture because it is a book that has long been found in plentiful supply in Saudi Arabia, and was a book that his father had in his home.

A few examples I documented from the Saudi textbooks for the higher grades, follow:

1. "The Jews and the Christians are enemies of the believers, and they cannot approve of Muslims."

2. "The struggle of this [Muslim] nation with the Jews and Christians has endured, and it will continue as long as God wills."

3. "Do not kill what God has forbidden killing such as the Muslim or the infidel between whom and the Muslims there is a covenant or under protection, unless for just cause such as unbelief after belief, just punishment or adultery."

4. "The apostate has two punishments; worldly and in the hereafter. Punishment in this life: Death if he does not repent."

5. "Major polytheism is a reason to fight those that practice it."

6. "Major polytheism makes [the taking of] blood and wealth permissible."

7. "Fighting the Infidels and the Polytheists has certain conditions and controls, including: That they be invited to Islam and they refuse to enter it and refuse to pay Jizya [a special tax] That Muslims have the power and the capacity to combat, That this be with the permission of the guardian and under his banner, That there be no guarantee between them and the Muslims not to combat."

8. "The punishment of homosexuality is death. . . . Ibn Qudamah said: "The companions (of the Prophet) agreed unanimously on killing. Some of the Companions argued that he (a homosexual) is to be burned with fire. It has been said that he should be stoned, or thrown from a high place. Other things have also been said."

9. "In Islamic law, (jihad) has two uses: 1. specific usage: which means: Exerting effort in fighting unbelievers and tyrants."

10. "In the general usage, Jihad is divided into the following categories: . . . Wrestling with the unbelievers by calling them (to the faith) and fighting them."

11. "As was cited in Ibn Abbas, and was said: The Apes are the people of the Sabbath, the Jews; and the Swine are the infidels of the communion of Jesus, the Christians."

12. "You can hardly find an example of sedition in which the Jews have not played a role."

13. "For since the Jews were scattered sundries they never knew peace with a single nation because of their proclivity for deceit, lying and conspiracy. Nothing proves this more than the Muslims' experience with them in Medina as the Prophet (PBUH) deported them and recommended that they be driven out from the Arabian Peninsula and as happened with them in other countries such as Germany, Poland, Spain and others."

14. "It is part of God's wisdom that the struggle between the Muslims and the Jews should continue until the hour [of judgment] The good news for Muslims is that God will help them against the Jews in the end."

15. "The whole [Muslim] nation lives in a Jihad against international Zionism manifested by the State of Jewish gangs' called Israel established on the land of Palestine wrongfully and in transgression."

To be sure the textbook language varies from year to year, and some intolerant passages have been word smithed, moved to later grades, repeated less often in the curriculum, paired with contradictory tolerant teachings and otherwise toned down. For example, last year's textbooks only instruct one way, by stoning, to kill a homosexual, instead of three, as before. Students are instructed to "hate the polytheists and the infidels" but, incongruously and without explanation, not to treat the infidels "unjustly," and, in a higher grade, taught four "reasons for hostility toward the kuffar (unbeliever)." Holy war is still extolled but now a ruler must decide when to make the call for jihad. The ideology of hatred and violence toward the "other" continued to be reflected in the textbooks of the last academic year.

Posted on the Internet and shipped worldwide, these texts are linked to growing extremism. Top U.S. Treasury counterterrorism officials have called the Wahhabi teachings of these textbooks "kindling for Bin Laden's match," and warned that, without education reform, "we will forever be faced with the challenge of disrupting the next group of terrorist facilitators and supporters." Most damning is the *New York Times* report that Saudi texts were used by ISIS in Mosul's schools. Indeed, Saudi high school students were studying from a textbook teaching that Muslims have an obligation to kill sorcerers even as ISIS posted a video this spring showing its militants in Egypt carrying out this directive – by beheading two elderly "sorcerers," probably Sufi Muslims, since such terms are loosely defined.

Complete Reform Is Always Just Around the Corner

In Riyadh, the other Commissioners and I met with the then-Saudi minister of education, Prince Faisal Bin Abdullah Bin Muhammad al-Saud. Like virtually every Saudi official who is asked, he acknowledged that 1–12 textbook reform was needed. But, he indicated that higher education, not high school, reform was then the government's priority. As confirmed in the State's religious freedom report, his office asserted to us that the math, science and English textbooks in 1st, 4th and 7th grades were given priority for revision, but these texts have not posed the greatest threats. He told us that he had a five-year plan for complete textbook reform. That meant that the high school textbooks would have been cleaned up by 2016 but they were not. As the 2017 State Department's human rights report on Saudi Arabia notes:

> The government's multi-year Tatweer project to revise textbooks, curricula, and teaching methods to promote tolerance and remove content disparaging religions other than Islam began in 2007. As of 2013, the program had received more than 11 billion riyals ($2.9 billion) to revise the curriculum, and the government had developed new curricula and textbooks for at least grades four through 10. *Despite these efforts, some intolerant material remained in textbooks used in schools.*(emphasis added)

This is not the first time that the Saudi government has obfuscated and broken its textbook reform promises to the U.S. government. On July 19, 20006, I was personally briefed about a new promise of reform by the State Department's ambassador for religious freedom. As a State Department press release announced, in a diplomatic "confirmation of policy," the Saudi government promised the United States complete educational reform by 2008. It asserted:

> The Saudi Government is conducting a comprehensive revision of textbooks and educational curricula to weed out disparaging remarks toward religious groups, a process that will be completed in one to two years.

Over a decade later, the process has yet to be completed. Moreover, the education minister told our commission delegation in 2011 that he was not aware of any such commitment.

Saudi Arabia's baleful reassurances of textbook reform date back even further to when its ambassador to Washington, Prince Turki al Faisal, in addition to taking out full page ads in American publications touting reform, stated at a Town Hall meeting in Los Angeles that:

> The Kingdom has reviewed all of its education practices and materials, and has removed any element that is inconsistent with the needs of a modern education. Not only have we eliminated what might be perceived as intolerance from old textbooks that were in our system, we have implemented a comprehensive internal revision and modernization plan.

When I later met with Ambassador Turki to show him my report findings on his government textbooks, he told me he had not personally read the textbooks and acknowledged that reform was still needed.

Periodically throughout these years, the Saudi government, with the help of a powerful public relations effort in Washington, has announced initiatives that were said to indicate resolve for textbook reform: the appointment of a woman director to the education department, the appointment of purported liberals as education ministers, a textbook pilot programs, the opening of a dialogue center in Vienna, Austria, teacher training programs, tolerance workshops and a "deradicalization" re-education program. It is difficult not to conclude that these efforts have been largely distractions that served to pull the wool over our eyes and failed to get at the heart of the problem –that is, eradicating the violent bigotry being actively promoted by the Saudi government in its textbooks. In March, Saudi Education Minister Issa announced plans to stop altogether the printing of textbooks within two or three years and to digitize them instead for wider accessibility. Whether or how this will impact the content of the religious texts is not clear.

Last year, the new Crown Prince Mohammed bin Salman made new promises to improve education, outlined in "National Transformation Program 2020." It contains plans to strengthen basic reading, math and science skills but gives little indication as to whether the state's religious textbooks will be reformed.

U.S. Government's Failure to Verify

The State Department has long treated the subject of Saudi Arabia's textbooks with kid gloves. Each year, these textbooks directing religious hatred, violence and war indoctrinate six million Saudi students and reach untold millions of others as they are spread far and wide in the Muslim world by a state that claims moral authority as the custodian of Islam's holiest sites. Yet, their role in advancing Islamist extremist ideology has not be taken seriously as a U.S. national security concern. Since 9/11, the State Department has barely raised the issue and at times has even worked to cover up their toxic content. It has not held the Saudi government to its repeated promises to the United States to reform its textbooks.

Since 2003, the State Department's some 1,000-page reports on human rights and religious freedom have contained a mere few lines each year on the Saudi textbooks. While blandly stating in boilerplate fashion, "some intolerant material remained in textbooks," they have routinely given assurances that reform is progressing. (A notable exception has been the reporting of the special envoy against anti-Semitism, which provided specific examples pertaining it this topic.) Assertions that reform was completed in a book authored by a former U.S. secretary of state also contributed to creating a false public perception that the Saudi textbooks no longer contain lessons that could be endangering American security and Middle Eastern stability.

The State Department once contracted the International Center on Religion & Diplomacy to evaluate the Saudi textbooks for the 2011-2012 academic year. The resulting report was promptly marked "classified" by the State Department and only became available to the public on June 29, 2016, by virtue of the Freedom of Information Act. By then, the Saudis could dismiss its findings on the basis it was out of date, four textbook editions having had replaced the one examined by the center. On another occasion, while I was a commissioner, the U.S. Commission on International Religious Freedom sent a delegation to Saudi Arabia, where it initiated a request for a set of the textbooks (which at that time were difficult to obtain) but, when, the requested texts arrived at the State Department, the U.S. International Religious Freedom Ambassador refused to release them, either to the commission or publicly.

Recommendations

Two months ago in Saudi Arabia, President Trump delivered a major speech before a gathering of fifty Saudi and other government leaders, laying out a new foreign policy strategy addressing terror. In it, the United States officially recognized – for the first time – that there is an ideology of "Islamist extremism" behind the terror attacks proliferating worldwide. The President pleaded with Muslim leaders to begin "honestly confronting the crisis of Islamist extremism and the Islamist terror groups it inspires." He declared that "Muslim nations must be willing to take on the burden, if we are going to defeat terrorism and send its wicked ideology into oblivion." He urged that we unite against "the murder of innocent Muslims, the oppression of women, the persecution of Jews, and the slaughter of Christians."

The president's words require new policies to be given effect. Five recommendations aimed at Saudi textbook reform follow:

1. The State Department should be mandated to review and publicly report annually on contemporaneous editions of Saudi government's textbooks, particularly the high school religious texts. These reports should point out intolerant passages that could negatively impact American citizens and interests.

2. American defense contracts with Saudi Arabia should be halted as long as the Saudi government publishes, posts, approves, finances or distributes textbooks that direct violence and hatred against any religion or group that may include American citizens.

3. The United States government should apply the range of diplomatic measures, including targeted visa denials to its government officials and their families, to press Saudi Arabia, at long last, to remove intolerant passages from school textbooks and other educational materials.

4. The State Department should report on the extent of the distribution of Saudi textbooks and education materials, including those distributed by the Saudi Department of Islamic Affairs, throughout the world.

5. Saudi Arabia should also be pressed to generally end its policies of religious persecution, as detailed in the State Department's religious freedom reports and the reports of the U.S. Commission on International Religious Freedom.

Mr. POE. Thank you, Ms. Shea.

Dr. Weinberg.

STATEMENT OF DAVID A. WEINBERG, PH.D., SENIOR FELLOW, FOUNDATION FOR DEFENSE OF DEMOCRACIES

Mr. WEINBERG. Chairman Poe, Ranking Member Keating, and distinguished members of the subcommittee, thank you on behalf of the Foundation for Defense of Democracies for having me here today. I will deliver an abridged version of my written testimony.

As I explain in that text, encouraging Saudi Arabia to remove incitement from its government-published textbooks for its public education system is not just the right thing to do, it is also a national security issue. Fighting terrorists militarily can only achieve so much if Saudi textbooks and other sources of incitement continue to provide fertile intellectual ground for violent extremism.

This past May I published a long list of intolerant statements in Saudi textbooks from the most current school year, which I will draw from extensively here. I have included all of these passages in their original Arabic as an appendix to my written testimony.

I found that Saudi textbooks still recommend killing people for many acts that U.S. law would characterize as personal choices. That included adultery, anal sex, converting from Islam, or purported acts of sorcery.

The textbooks are also rife with anti-Christian and particularly anti-Semitic inciting, often framed as anti-Zionism. One book called Christianity an invalid, perverted religion. Another accused Zionism of plotting a global Jewish government. And a third called Zionism an octopus that it accused, falsely, of trying to destroy the Al Aqsa Mosque and the entire Islamic creed.

A fourth book taught that befriending infidels is forbidden, citing a Quranic verse that says not to take Christians or Jews as allies. That textbook called such infidels enemies of Muslims and of God, and taught that Muslims must abhor them, quite literally teaching hatred.

These are all examples from current textbooks used in the 2016 to 2017 Saudi school year.

According to a forthcoming report by Human Rights Watch, the textbooks also repeatedly refer to well-known stereotypes of Shiite or Sufi Muslim rituals as horrendous examples of polytheism. This is particularly important, because a passage I found in a current Saudi textbook called for fighting such polytheists except under a handful of extenuating circumstances.

That book also teaches that there are four types of infidels, and that if a non-believer doesn't happen to fit into one of the first three categories—diplomats, peoples with whom Muslims have a non-aggression treaty, or people who agree to pay a special tax associated with second class status—then they are combatant whom it says Muslims are commanded to fight.

Saudi Arabia has made some positive changes to its textbooks in recent years but not enough. A few passages condemning terrorism or racism and permitting kind treatment to peaceful non-believers have been added. Direct calls to violence or hatred are somewhat less common.

By the way, I would like to share a little bit of news with you today. Seventeen minutes after this hearing was scheduled to start the Saudi Embassy posted on Twitter that, "The Ministry of Education has finalized a round of textbook revisions in line with the objectives of the national transformation plan." This is particularly puzzling because in an interview with the Wall Street Journal earlier this year Saudi Arabia's education minister seemed to suggest that the broader change involving incitement and other issues in its curriculum would have to wait until 3 years, up to 3 years from now when the Kingdom would move to tablets in the classroom.

Saudi officials routinely oversell the success and ambition of their efforts to reform these books to date. In 2005 Saudi Arabia said it had removed all the problematic passages from its textbooks. When Nina Shea proved that that was incorrect, the Saudis assured the U.S. that all intolerant passages would be removed by 2008. They missed that deadline, as well as others they had pledged for 2013, 2014, 2015, and 2016. Even some of the textbooks they claim to have fixed in recent years still contain incitement.

U.S. policy on this issue has not been up to the task. For example, the State Department issued the country reports on counterterrorism today. And while there are several lines in there about the Saudi curriculum, there is only half, less than a full sentence on what incitement still remains.

But there is much that Congress can do to help. The U.S. Commission on International Religious Freedom called on the executive branch this year to "undertake and make public an annual assessment" of Saudi textbooks to "determine if passages that teach religious intolerance had been removed." Congress should help by passing legislation that requires the administration to issue such a yearly report, and allocates the resources of it to do so, no later than 90 days after the start of the Saudi school year so such findings are actually still valid for diplomats. And such a report should quote all such passages that could be seen as encouraging violence or intolerance for public scrutiny.

There are a number of other recommendations that I include in my written testimony. But in the interests of time, I will leave off there.

[The prepared statement of Mr. Weinberg follows:]

CONGRESSIONAL TESTIMONY: FOUNDATION FOR DEFENSE OF DEMOCRACIES

House Committee on Foreign Affairs
Terrorism, Non-Proliferation, and Trade Subcommittee

Saudi Arabia's Troubling Educational Curriculum

DAVID ANDREW WEINBERG, PH.D.

Senior Fellow
Foundation for Defense of Democracies

Washington, DC
July 19, 2017

www.defenddemocracy.org

David Andrew Weinberg   July 19, 2017

Chairman Poe, Ranking Member Keating, and distinguished Members of the Subcommittee, thank you on behalf of the Foundation for Defense of Democracies for the opportunity to testify before you today about incitement in Saudi Arabia's government-published textbooks for school children. It is an honor to be back, particularly because I first engaged with Saudi Arabia on this issue as a staff member for this body's full committee.

Half a decade after 9/11, Nina Shea wrote in an outstanding Freedom House report that Saudi officials accepted their textbooks had problems but "have repeatedly pledged that reform is underway or completed."[1] That is still the case today.[2]

Yet as the author of the most recent published study on incitement remaining in Saudi textbooks today,[3] I can vouch that over a decade later Riyadh *still* has not persuasively shown that this problem has been resolved.

Unfortunately, U.S. policy has not been up to the task of convincing our Saudi allies to remove this incitement with greater urgency.

For example, I exposed in a 2014 monograph that the State Department appeared to have allocated half a million dollars in taxpayer funds to commission a two-part study on Saudi textbooks that was intended for public release but was instead withheld to avoid embarrassing the Saudis or the U.S. administration.[4] Its detailed findings were hidden from public scrutiny for years[5] and only raised with the Saudis at a senior level after the textbooks it had evaluated were already out of date.[6]

In the testimony that follows, I will argue that this is particularly disturbing because incitement of this sort is not just a moral issue or a human rights issue, it is a national security issue. While Saudi

---

[1] Nina Shea, "Saudi Arabia's Curriculum of Intolerance: With Excerpts from Saudi Ministry of Education Textbooks for Islamic Studies," *Freedom House*, 2006, page 11. (https://freedomhouse.org/sites/default/files/CurriculumOfIntolerance.pdf)

[2] Margherita Stancati and Ahmed Al Omran, "Saudis Ready Digital Push to Get Islamic Extremism out of Schools: Textbooks were Criticized after 9/11 for Tendentious Content Pitting Muslims against Other Religions," *The Wall Street Journal*, February 15, 2017. (https://www.wsj.com/articles/saudis-ready-digital-push-to-get-islamic-extremism-out-of-schools-1487154603)

[3] David Andrew Weinberg, "Trump's Counter-Extremism Effort Should Address Saudi Textbooks: The President Will Have to Address Incitement in Riyadh's Government-Published Textbooks," *The Huffington* Post, May 20, 2017. (http://www.huffingtonpost.com/entry/turning-the-page-on-hate-trumps-counter-extremism_us_5920a45de4b0c8f558bb2719)

[4] David Andrew Weinberg, "Textbook Diplomacy: Why the State Department Shelved a Study on Incitement in Saudi Education Materials," *Foundation for Defense of Democracies*, March 2014. (http://www.defenddemocracy.org/content/uploads/documents/Textbook_Diplomacy.pdf)

[5] "The State of Tolerance in the Curriculum of the Kingdom of Saudi Arabia," *International Center for Religion and Diplomacy*, 2012, page 104. (https://www.nytimes.com/interactive/2016/08/17/international-home/document-state-dept-study-on-saudi-textbooks.html); "The Global Spread of Saudi Textbooks," *International Center for Religion and Diplomacy*, 2013. (https://www.nytimes.com/interactive/2016/08/17/international-home/document-state-dept-study-on-saudi-textbooks.html)

[6] David Andrew Weinberg, "Textbook Diplomacy: Why the State Department Shelved a Study on Incitement in Saudi Education Materials," *Foundation for Defense of Democracies*, March 2014, pages 4 and 8. (http://www.defenddemocracy.org/content/uploads/documents/Textbook_Diplomacy.pdf)

textbooks are not the only significant source of incitement from the Gulf – or even in Saudi Arabia – they are an important bellwether and concern for U.S. policy.

I will then endeavor to present everything we know about incitement in the latest edition of Saudi Arabia's official textbooks. Examples of such incitement include: (1) directives to kill people in response to their non-violent personal life choices, (2) messages that are undoubtedly anti-Semitic or anti-Christian, (3) lessons that are intolerant toward adherents of non-monotheistic religions as well as implicitly toward Shiite and Sufi Muslims, and (4) several other passages encouraging violence.

I will explain how Riyadh regularly oversells the success of its textbook reforms. I will then argue for why U.S. policy in this regard needs to change urgently. Next, I will refute some common counterarguments by those who claim that U.S. pressure cannot have a positive impact on the Saudi curriculum. Finally, I will conclude by offering a list of policy recommendations for Congress which could help encourage the Saudi government to address this issue in a more effective and timely manner.

I. The Books are a National Security Issue

Addressing incitement in Saudi Arabia's government-published textbooks is important for several different reasons. First of all, speaking out when hatred is being spread is simply the right thing to do. It is a barometer of how seriously any U.S. administration takes the fight against anti-Semitism and protecting Christians and vulnerable Muslim minorities abroad.[7] It is an important avenue for toning down sectarian hatred in the Middle East without taking the side of Iran's terror-sponsoring regime. And it is a basic human rights issue.

But most importantly, addressing incitement in Saudi Arabia, including in textbooks, is a serious national security issue. Saudi society has been a top source of foreign terrorist fighters – and, at times, terrorist leaders – in places like Iraq and Syria.[8] Saudi Arabia was the original home of Osama bin Laden, and fifteen of the nineteen hijackers on 9/11 were Saudi nationals. While Saudi authorities have reportedly convicted hundreds of defendants on terror finance charges,[9] they still grapple with the enormous challenge of radicalized private individuals seeking to fund terrorist groups.[10]

---

[7] See, for example. "AJC Urges U.S. to Press Saudis on Textbooks." *American Jewish Committee*. March 26, 2014. (http://www.ajc.org/site/apps/nlnet/content2.aspx?c=7oJILSPwFfISG&b=8479733&ct=13805419)

[8] Ned Parker. "Iraqi Insurgency Said to Include Many Saudis: They Outnumber other Foreigners, and Half Join as Suicide Bombers, a Senior U.S. Officer Says," *Los Angeles Times*, July 15, 2007. (http://articles.latimes.com/2007/jul/15/world/fg-saudi15); Mohanad Hashim, "Iraq and Syria: Who are the Foreign Fighters?" *BBC News* (UK), September 3. 2014. (http://www.bbc.com/news/world-middle-east-29043331); "The Other Beheaders: Crime and Punishment in Saudi Arabia," *The Economist*, September 20, 2014. (https://www.economist.com/news/middle-east-and-africa/21618918-possible-reasons-mysterious-surge-executions-other-beheaders)

[9] Financial Action Task Force, "Terrorist Financing FATF Report to G20 Leaders: Actions Being Taken by the FATF," November 2015, page 4. (http://www.fatf-gafi.org/media/fatf/documents/reports/Terrorist-financing-actions-taken-by-FATF.pdf)

[10] Declan Walsh, "Wikileaks Cables Portray Saudi Arabia as a Cash Machine for Terrorists." *The Guardian* (UK), December 5, 2010. (https://www.theguardian.com/world/2010/dec/05/wikileaks-cables-saudi-terrorist-funding); David Andrew Weinberg, "Analysis: State Department Identifies Gulf Shortcomings on Counterterrorism Efforts,"

David Andrew Weinberg

July 19, 2017

The kingdom's books have emerged in well over a dozen countries over the years, including Algeria, Austria, Burkina Faso, China, Comoros, Djibouti, France, Indonesia, Nigeria, Pakistan, Somalia, Tanzania, Thailand, the United Kingdom, and previously the United States.[11] The valedictorian of a school in Virginia that had used the textbooks was convicted in 2005 of plotting with al-Qaeda to assassinate President George W. Bush.[12]

Until 2015, Saudi textbooks were even the curriculum of choice in territory held by the Islamic State, according to the *New York Times*.[13] Much like those books recommended, the Islamic State executed numerous individuals on suspicion of homosexuality, insulting Allah or the Prophet Muhammad, adultery, or purported sorcery.[14]

Saudi textbooks are the most pivotal ones from a national security perspective, due to what author Robert Lacey explains is an accident of history regarding how the kingdom was established. The Saudi kingdom, founded in 1932, brought together disparate elements from three different regions: (1) the austere religious traditions of central Saudi Arabia, (2) the oil wealth of Saudi Arabia's Eastern Province, and (3) the mantle of religious legitimacy from controlling the two holiest sites in Islam, in Saudi Arabia's west. This fusion allowed Saudi rulers to lavishly and persuasively promote their brand of Islam, first within the kingdom and then beyond.[15]

When Stuart Levey was the U.S. Treasury Department's under secretary for terrorism and financial intelligence, he wrote that fighting indoctrination such as intolerant textbooks is "even more important" than cutting off terrorist finance. He explained that unless we stop the indoctrination of future generations, America "will forever be faced with the challenge of disrupting the next group of terrorist facilitators and supporters."[16]

FDD's Long War Journal, June 3, 2016. (http://www.longwarjournal.org/archives/2016/06/analysis-state-department-identifies-gulf-shortcomings-on-counterterrorism-efforts.php)

[11] International Center for Religion and Diplomacy, "The Global Spread of Saudi Textbooks." 2013. (https://www.nytimes.com/interactive/2016/08/17/international-home/document-state-dept-study-on-saudi-textbooks.html); Graham Paton, "Muslim Pupils Learn to Cut Off Hands of Thieves," *The Telegraph* (UK), November 21, 2010. (http://www.telegraph.co.uk/education/educationnews/8150247/Muslim-pupils-learn-to-cut-off-hands-of-thieves.html); "Saudi School 'Teaching Anti-Semitism'," *The Local* (Austria), November 14, 2014. (https://www.thelocal.at/20141114/saudi-school-teaching-anti-semitism): Jamie Tarabay, "Virginia Islamic School's Expansion Met Protests," *NPR*, January 30, 2010. (http://www.npr.org/templates/story/story.php?storyId=122987391)

[12] Jerry Markon, "Va. Man's Sentence Increased to Life in Terror Plot," *The Washington Post*, July 28, 2009. (http://www.washingtonpost.com/wp-dyn/content/article/2009/07/27/AR2009072701384.html)

[13] David D. Kirkpatrick, "ISIS' Harsh Brand of Islam is Rooted in Austere Saudi Creed," *The New York Times*, September 24, 2014. (https://www.nytimes.com/2014/09/25/world/middleeast/isis-abu-bakr-baghdadi-caliph-wahhabi.html?partner=rss&emc=rss&smid=tw-nytimes&_r=1); Scott Shane, "Saudis and Extremism: 'Both the Arsonists and the Firefighters,'" *The New York Times*, August 25, 2016. (https://www.nytimes.com/2016/08/26/world/middleeast/saudi-arabia-islam.html)

[14] See, for example, Syrian Observatory for Human Rights, "103 People Executed in 7 Provinces over 50 Days," *Syrian Observatory for Human Rights*, February 20, 2015. (http://www.syriahr.com/en/?p=13059); David Andrew Weinberg, "Saudi Textbooks Propagate Intolerance," *The Hill*, October 30, 2015. (http://thehill.com/blogs/congress-blog/education/258583-saudi-textbooks-propagate-intolerance)

[15] Robert Lacey, *Inside the Kingdom: Kings, Clerics, Modernists, Terrorists, and the Struggle for Saudi Arabia* (Penguin, 2009), pages xx-xxi.

[16] Stuart A. Levey, "Loss of Moneyman a Big Blow for al-Qaeda," *The Washington Post*, June 6, 2010. (http://www.washingtonpost.com/wp-dyn/content/article/2010/06/04/AR2010060404271.html)

David Andrew Weinberg

Tom Farr, a former director of the State Department's International Religious Freedom, was even more explicit. In 2008, he argued that the U.S. government's lack of urgency and failure to hold Riyadh to its own deadlines for fixing the textbooks and other promised religious freedom reforms meant that "the primary 'lesson' of 9/11 [was] shunted to the side."[17] Indeed, without urgently addressing the religious incitement that provides fertile intellectual ground for such violent extremism, we may unfortunately be fated to keep repeating the past.

Saudi Arabia today is not the worst country in the Gulf when it comes to state-backed incitement. That title goes to the government of Iran, which regularly calls for the annihilation of Israel and viciously dehumanizes its enemies.[18] Qatar's record is also as bad or worse than Saudi Arabia's when it comes to the extremist messages that are propagated by its state-backed media and by state-backed preachers.[19] But because Saudi Arabia is so much bigger than Qatar, the impact of what it teaches to school children at home is felt around the world.

Textbooks are also not the only challenge involving incitement in Saudi Arabia, but they are the most obvious bellwether for assessing issues of this sort. When the Education Ministry itself adopts certain extremist messages, puts them in writing, and teaches them to children, the link that runs from the state to such incitement is particularly meaningful. While the U.S. should seek to address other areas of incitement as well – such as by Saudi government officials[20] and by state-backed preachers[21] – the kingdom's textbooks are a very important indicator of its conduct and intentions.

II. Accessing the Latest Books

Oren Adaki and I worked together at FDD on the issue of Saudi textbooks during the 2013-2014 school year. He did path-breaking work on those books at the time,[22] and I am thrilled to see him serving as the staff director for this subcommittee today. For the subsequent two school years, however, two of the main online venues for accessing the books were made password protected, effectively blocking foreigners.[23] The senior Saudi officials whom I contacted in this regard declined to grant me access.

---

[17] Thomas F. Farr, *World of Faith and Freedom: Why International Religious Liberty is Vital to American National Security* (Oxford, 2008), page 241.

[18] Michael Gerson, "Iran's Hate Speech is an Incitement to Genocide," *The Washington Post*, April 4, 2013. (https://www.washingtonpost.com/opinions/michael-gerson-irans-hate-speech-is-an-incitement-to-genocide/2013/04/04/2686e7a8-9ca1-11e2-9a79-eb5280c81c63_story.html?utm_term=.d4b95d66e89e)

[19] David Andrew Weinberg, "Congress Must Press Qatar for Highlighting Hate Preacher," *The Hill*, April 30, 2017. (http://thehill.com/blogs/pundits-blog/foreign-policy/331264-congress-must-press-qatar-for-highlighting-hate-preacher)

[20] David Daoud and David Andrew Weinberg, "Two Steps Forward, One Step Back: Saudi Arabia Still Hostile to Jews," *The Forward*, May 15, 2017. (http://www.defenddemocracy.org/media-hit/david-daoud-two-steps-forward-one-step-back-saudi-arabia-still-hostile-to-israel/)

[21] David Daoud and David Andrew Weinberg, "Saudi Clerics' Rhetoric – and Implications for Global Security," *The Wall Street Journal*, April 20, 2016. (https://blogs.wsj.com/washwire/2016/04/20/saudi-clerics-rhetoric-and-implications-for-global-security/)

[22] Oren Adaki, "Highlighting Hatred in Saudi Textbooks," *Foundation for Defense of Democracies website*, March 27, 2014. (http://www.defenddemocracy.org/media-hit/oren-adaki-highlighting-hatred-in-saudi-textbooks/)

[23] iTunes app "المناهج الدراسية" accessed July 14, 2017. (https://goo.gl/qk4SBk); "بوابة المحتوى الرقمي للمناهج" accessed July 14, 2017; archived April 10, 2016. (https://goo.gl/wo2kvU); "بوابة المحتوى الرقمي للمناهج" accessed July 14, 2017; archived July 8, 2016. (https://goo.gl/2MZs8A)

David Andrew Weinberg   July 19, 2017

Accessing Saudi Arabia's government-published textbooks has been a recurring challenge not just for American researchers, but also for U.S. government officials. When the State Department undertook a 2006 in-house study of several textbooks at the U.S. Embassy in Riyadh, it "borrowed" books from school children because the host government did not answer repeated requests for the books.[24] When the International Center for Religion and Diplomacy (ICRD) was conducting a review of Saudi textbooks on behalf of the U.S. government, it said religious studies textbooks for grades three and six "were regrettably unobtainable."[25] On several occasions, the U.S. Commission on International Religious Freedom was promised textbooks by Saudi officials, wrote letters to follow up, and received no reply.[26] Other times, the websites recommended by Riyadh to U.S. officials for accessing the books were out of service or incomplete.[27]

But in early 2017, I received an invaluable tip that many, if not all, of the Education Ministry-published books for the 2016-2017 school year were now available at a different location that was not password protected – a website maintained by the state-chartered corporation for curriculum modernization.[28] To the best of my knowledge, books for the 2017-2018 school year have not yet been released, so these are still the most up-to-date books for use in Saudi public schools.

I conducted a study of key selections from those 2016-2017 books, looking primarily at those textbooks in which religious incitement had previously been a major problem (especially high school books on religious matters).[29] I published the results of that study as an article for the *Huffington Post*, from which I have drawn extensively here.[30] For each passage from those textbooks that I reference here, I have included at the end of this testimony a copy of that book's cover page, copyright page, and the page(s) on which that passage occurred. At two other points in this section, I cite textbook studies by other authors; in those instances, I reference and footnote their studies explicitly.

---

[24] David Andrew Weinberg, "Textbook Diplomacy: Why the State Department Shelved a Study on Incitement in Saudi Education Materials," *Foundation for Defense of Democracies*. March 2014, page 7. (http://www.defenddemocracy.org/content/uploads/documents/Textbook_Diplomacy.pdf)

[25] "The State of Tolerance in the Curriculum of the Kingdom of Saudi Arabia," International Center for Religion and Diplomacy, 2012, page 104. (https://www.nytimes.com/interactive/2016/08/17/international-home/document-state-dept-study-on-saudi-textbooks.html)

[26] U.S. Commission on International Religious Freedom, "Policy Focus: Saudi Arabia," Fall 2007, pages 2, 6, 13-14, and 22. (http://www.uscirf.gov/sites/default/files/resources/stories/PDFs/PolicyFocus_SaudiArabia_Fall2007.pdf); U.S. Commission on International Religious Freedom, "Annual Report for 2010," May 2010, page 130. (http://www.uscirf.gov/sites/default/files/resources/ar2010/saudiarabia2010.pdf); U.S. Commission on International Religious Freedom, "Annual Report for 2011," May 2011, page 150. (http://www.uscirf.gov/sites/default/files/resources/book%20with%20cover%20for%20web.pdf)

[27] Nina Shea, *Ten Years On: Saudi Arabia's Textbooks Still Promote Religious Violence* (Hudson Institute, 2011), page 6. (https://www.hudson.org/content/researchattachments/attachment/931/sauditextbooks2011final.pdf); U.S. Commission on International Religious Freedom, "Annual Report 2013," April 2013, page 142. (http://www.uscirf.gov/sites/default/files/resources/2013%20USCIRF%20Annual%20Report%20(2).pdf)

[28] iEn National Education Portal, "التعليم العام" accessed July 14, 2017. (https://ien.edu.sa/#/home/5142)

[29] I received invaluable advice in this regard from David Daoud, who was serving as an Arabic-language research analyst at FDD and now works for United Against a Nuclear Iran.

[30] David Andrew Weinberg, "Trump's Counter-Extremism Effort Should Address Saudi Textbooks: The President Will Have to Address Incitement in Riyadh's Government-Published Textbooks," *The Huffington Post*. May 20, 2017. (http://www.huffingtonpost.com/entry/turning-the-page-on-hate-trumps-counter-extremism_us_5920a45de4b0e8f558bb2719)

David Andrew Weinberg   July 19, 2017

(A) Recommending the Death Penalty for Personal Life Choices

The latest editions of several Saudi textbooks call for the killing of any individual who engages in certain acts that we in the United States would treat as personal life choices. The lessons in these books are even harsher than how the Saudi state tends to approach such issues: Whereas judges often apply a strict evidentiary standard to reduce the likelihood of executing a defendant for such acts, no such mitigating context is provided in these lessons.

A 2016-2017 high school textbook on Islamic jurisprudence teaches that the punishment for adultery is being stoned to death. It adds that the penalty for premarital sex is one hundred lashes and a year of exile.

That same book defines anal sex as a "crime" and says that the majority of jurists have determined that the penalty for it is "like the penalty for adultery," meaning death. The book dehumanizes anybody who engages in such an act, teaching that it "creates depravity and lowliness in the soul of whoever commits it, since it extinguishes life." The book adds that societies in which anal sex spreads are swiftly punished by God, incurring disasters, plagues, iniquity, and corruption.

Additionally, the book teaches that adultery, premarital, and anal sex each bring shame upon one's family and tribe. This is a key element of the belief system that can lead to tragic honor killings in some communities.

This introductory book on religious law also mandates the death penalty for what is calls "apostasy," meaning abandoning or renouncing Islam. The book teaches that anybody who does not "return to his religion" after three days must be killed and will then spend an "eternity in fire." The lesson teaches that there are three main kinds of apostasy: (1) "mocking Allah or his prophet or his religion" and praying to an entity other than Allah, (2) drawing closer to an entity other than Allah in ritual acts, or (3) belief in something known to be forbidden in Islam, such as permitting the consumption of alcohol.

Lastly, the 2016-2017 Saudi curriculum teaches that the death penalty should be applied for certain perceived acts of sorcery, according to an introductory high school book on monotheism. For those involved in what it calls devil magic, the penalty given is execution by the state. For acts of magical sleight of hand, the instructed penalty is a rebuke that it says can also go up to the level of execution.

It is also worth noting that this is the only one of the four directives listed here that specifies that the killing of such people must be carried out by an authority appointed by the ruler. In all other instances, that assessment is left up to interpretation by the reader, which could leave open the possibility of vigilante violence by non-state groups.

(B) Anti-Semitic and Anti-Christian Messages

A 2016-2017 Saudi textbook for high school students on *Hadith* – the traditional corpus of actions attributed to the Prophet Muhammad – teaches some rather problematic messages about present-

David Andrew Weinberg   July 19, 2017

day Christianity. The book alleges that "Christianity in its current state is an invalid, perverted religion" whose promoters seek to dominate Muslim nations using the "weapon" of "intellectual invasion." The book falsely alleges that the American Universities in Cairo and Beirut are two of "the institutions leading Christianization all over the world" today.

That same textbook also teaches some misleading lessons about Zionism, the movement to establish a national home for the Jewish people. It baselessly alleges that Zionism aspires to world domination and a "global Jewish government." It falsely argues that – as a prelude to world domination – the aim of present-day Zionism and the Israeli government is to establish a Greater Israel that stretches from the Nile to the Euphrates.

Similarly, a 2016-2017 high school social studies book from Saudi Arabia calls Zionism an "octopus" that it falsely accuses of seeking to destroy the al-Aqsa Mosque and the entire "Islamic creed." It should be noted that imagery of global Jewry as an octopus is a common trope used in other anti-Semitic hoaxes, including some editions of the *Protocols of the Elders of Zion*,[31] Henry Ford's *The International Jew*,[32] and Nazi propaganda.[33]

These books single out Zionism among all other self-determination movements as inherently racist and expansionist, inexplicably accusing it of spreading drugs and sexually-transmitted diseases in Islamic countries. The books also present Zionism as inherently "hostile" and a "threat" to the Arab and Muslim world.

In a lesson entitled "the Intifada and the Zionist threat," one of them also falsely asserts that the first Palestinian intifada caused roughly a million Jews to emigrate from Israel. It praises the intifada as "a war sapping the wave of the Zionists" and as "a preparation for liberation, Allah permitting."

A twelfth-grade textbook on monotheism from 2016-2017 teaches that God "forbade befriending the infidels," in part based on a Quranic verse it includes that says not to take Jews or Christians as allies. The book alleges three reasons for this prohibition, asserting that such infidels are "enemies of God," "enemies of Islam" and its adherents, and that befriending them would show support for disbelief.

That lesson also teaches that a key part of Islam and Muslim relations with non-believers is a requirement to "abhor the enemies of Allah and their hostilities."

(C) Messages against Sufi and Shiite Rituals and Non-Monotheistic Religions

---

[31] "Egyptian Television Re-Airs Anti-Semitic Miniseries 'Horseman without a Horse,'" *Anti-Defamation League*, April 5, 2012. (https://www.adl.org/blog/egyptian-television-re-airs-anti-semitic-miniseries-horseman-without-a-horse)

[32] "File:2001 ed The International Jew by Henry Ford.jpg," *Wikipedia*, accessed July 14, 2017. (https://en.wikipedia.org/wiki/File:2001_ed_The_International_Jew_by_Henry_Ford.jpg)

[33] "'Seppla' [Josef Plank], Churchill as an Octopus, between 1935 and 1943," in *Churchill and the Great Republic*, accessed July 14, 2017 via Library of Congress. (http://www.loc.gov/exhibits/churchill/interactive/_html/wc0213.html)

David Andrew Weinberg					July 19, 2017

Saudi Arabia's strict brand of Salafist Sunni Islam, commonly referred to in the West as Wahhabism, maintains a strong emphasis on eschewing any religious practices that could be perceived as deviations from monotheism. As a result, the kingdom's curriculum includes numerous books on monotheism that admonish against acts of polytheism ("*shirk*") and its practitioners ("*mushrikeen*"). As such, these lessons are inherently critical toward adherents of non-monotheistic religions. They also single out for criticism many of the rituals that are commonly associated in the local context with Shiite or Sufi Islam.

For example, an eighth-grade Saudi textbook on monotheism from 2016-2017 that I found defines such rituals – such as praying while walking around a grave or shrine – as an act of polytheism. Alongside that passage in the text, the book presents a picture with a big "X" of what appears to be a mock-up of a shrine with names of several Shiite imams behind it.

In this regard, I would like to recommend to you an important forthcoming study by Human Rights Watch on systematic discrimination against Shiite citizens of Saudi Arabia.[34] In it, the organization examines how Saudi primary school textbooks on monotheism from 2016-2017 present relations with non-Sunni Muslims. Generally speaking, it finds that while the curriculum does not address Shiite Islam explicitly or employ a common local slur for its practitioners as "rejectionists," the books are still deeply problematic.

They discovered that the 2016-2017 books clearly endorsed Sunni Islam over other religions and repeatedly referred to well-known stereotypes of Shiite or Sufi rituals as horrendous examples of polytheism. Key examples of such rituals included swearing by or showing reverence for early figures in Shiite Islam, praying for these or other saintly figures to "intercede" with Allah on one's behalf, wailing over the dead as some Shiite Muslims do during the holy day of Ashura, and making pilgrimages to religious sites in addition to those in Mecca and Medina.

(D) Other Encouragement of Violence

The language in 2016-2017 Saudi textbooks that calls for killing people who engage in adultery, anal sex, apostasy, or certain supposed acts of sorcery are not the only passages that encourage violence against those who act in a manner inconsistent with the state's vision of Islam.

A 2016-2017 Saudi textbook on monotheism for the twelfth grade teaches that there are four kinds of infidels. The first three of them include envoys who have diplomatic immunity, peoples who have a non-aggression pact with the Muslim world, and *dhimmis*, a term for non-Muslims forced to pay a special tax that is commonly associated with second-class status. According to this book, the remainder of infidels, who comprise the fourth class, are defined as "combatants," whom it says Allah has commanded must be fought until they submit to Islam or agree to become *dhimmis*.

That book also calls for "fighting the infidels and the polytheists" except under a handful of extenuating circumstances. Those include: (1) if such non-Muslims have not been given a chance yet to convert to Islam or become *dhimmis*, (2) if Muslims are not strong enough to win such a fight, (3) if the ruler does not support it, or (4) if such non-Muslims have a non-aggression pact with the Muslim world.

---

[34] Human Rights Watch, *They Are Not Our Brothers: Hate Speech by Saudi Officials*, (forthcoming).

David Andrew Weinberg

July 19, 2017

According to a February 2017 *Wall Street Journal* article, a current eighth-grade Saudi textbook on Islamic law instructed readers to support people who are waging *jihad*, including by arming them. The passage was translated by the *Journal* as follows: "the *mujahideen* who are doing good deeds for the sake of Allah ... should be given transportation, weapons, food and anything else they may need to continue their jihad."[35]

III. Full Reform is Never Around the Corner

I recently was told by a credible source that Saudi officials now privately claim to have completed the wholesale removal of religious incitement from their curriculum for the upcoming (2017-2018) school year. Such claims would have to be viewed with great skepticism due to the kingdom's past track record.

In addition to missing several stated deadlines for textbook reform, Saudi authorities have routinely oversold the extent of these initiatives to date. As State Department officials have reportedly conceded in private, the real pace of Saudi textbook reform has been "glacial."[36] Three times in the last decade, newly-appointed Saudi education ministers were hailed by the West as reformers only to leave office without making meaningful strides toward resolving this issue.[37]

In 2003, Adel al-Jubeir – then an advisor to Saudi Arabia's crown prince and now the kingdom's foreign minister – told Tim Russert that the textbooks issue was "overblown," since the kingdom's books had already been "changed."[38]

In 2005, Saudi Arabia's then-foreign minister, Prince Saud al-Faisal, inaccurately assured an audience at the Council on Foreign Relations that "we have gone through a whole program of going into the educational system from top to bottom, from schools, teachers, books, and we have taken everything out of them that does not call for cooperation [and] coexistence."[39]

---

[35] Margherita Stancati and Ahmed Al Omran, "Saudis Ready Digital Push to Get Islamic Extremism out of Schools: Textbooks were Criticized after 9/11 for Tendentious Content Pitting Muslims against Other Religions," *The Wall Street Journal*, February 15, 2017. (https://www.wsj.com/articles/saudis-ready-digital-push-to-get-islamic-extremism-out-of-schools-1487154603); This newspaper article also included several other worrisome passages from Saudi textbooks, but there is some inconsistency in the piece as to whether those other passages were from the most recent school year or from previous editions.

[36] Cited in Nina Shea, *Ten Years On: Saudi Arabia's Textbooks Still Promote Religious Violence* (Hudson Institute, 2011). page 12. (https://www.hudson.org/content/researchattachments/attachment/931/sauditextbooks2011final.pdf)

[37] "Editorial: A Promise of Reform in Saudi Arabia," *The New York Times*, February 25, 2009. (http://www.nytimes.com/2009/02/26/opinion/26thu2.html); Ellen Knickmeyer and Ahmed Omran, "Some Saudis See New Appointments as Challenge to Kingdom's Fundamentalists," *The Wall Street Journal*, December 23, 2013. (https://blogs.wsj.com/middleeast/2013/12/23/some-saudis-see-new-appointments-as-challenge-to-kingdoms-fundamentalists/); "A New King's Duty to Young Saudis," *Christian Science Monitor*, February 4, 2015. (https://www.csmonitor.com/Commentary/the-monitors-view/2015/0204/A-new-king-s-duty-to-young-Saudis)

[38] Royal Embassy of Saudi Arabia, Press Release, "Adel al-Jubeir, Foreign Policy Advisor to Crown Prince Abdullah on NBC's 'Meet the Press'," May 18, 2003, archived June 12, 2015. (http://web.archive.org/web/20150612094516/https://saudiembassy.net/archive/2003/transcript/page21.aspx)

[39] "The Fight against Extremism and the Search for Peace," *Council on Foreign Relations*, September 20, 2005, archived April 19, 2017. (http://web.archive.org/web/20170419011341/https://www.cfr.org/radicalization-and-extremism/fight-against-extremism-search-peace-rush-transcript-federal-news-service-inc/p8908)

He was echoed by King Abdullah, who told Barbara Walters that fall that the kingdom had "toned ... down" its textbooks to limit their possible contribution to extremism.[40]

In the spring of 2006, Saudi Arabia's ambassador to the United States, Prince Turki al-Faisal, told a town hall in Los Angeles that "we eliminated what might be perceived as intolerance from old text books that were in our system," and he made similar remarks to an audience in Chicago as well.[41]

In July 2006, Saudi Arabia pledged to the U.S. government to "remove remaining intolerant references that disparage Muslims or non-Muslims or that promote hatred toward other religions or religious groups," and that it "expect[ed] to complete this process in one to two years."[42] Of course, that deadline was missed entirely, and the U.S. did little to chastise the Saudis for falling short.

In March 2008, Saudi Arabia's deputy minister of education in charge of textbook updates is reported to have incorrectly claimed to the U.S. Embassy that "most intolerant language had been removed" already from the kingdom's school books.[43]

This reported assertion is particularly surprising because the State Department later reported that his Education Ministry had just embarked in 2007 on a multi-year process of revising its textbooks, starting with some of the lower grades and planning to work their way up.[44] In effect, this involved focusing on what Douglas Johnston of ICRD once characterized as "low-hanging fruit,"[45] revising less controversial textbooks for the lower grades while saving the books with the most problematic materials, which were always at the high school level, for some point down the road.

According to the U.S. Commission on International Religious Freedom, Saudi officials claimed several years into this process that they had "thoroughly revised" the textbooks for these lower grades.[46] According to the State Department, Saudi Arabia's Ministry of Education said that

---

[40] "Transcript: Saudi King Abdullah Talks to Barbara Walters," *ABC News*, October 14, 2015.
(http://abcnews.go.com/2020/International/story?id=1214706&page=1)

[41] Royal Embassy of Saudi Arabia, Press Release, "Saudi Ambassador Addresses Town Hall Los Angeles, March 21, 2006, archived September 9, 2015.
(http://web.archive.org/web/20150909222625/https://saudiembassy.net/archive/2006/speeches/page52.aspx); Royal Embassy of Saudi Arabia, Press Release, "Prince Turki's Address to the Chicago Council on Foreign Relations," April 20, 2006, archived September 10, 2015.
(http://web.archive.org/web/20150910090029/https://saudiembassy.net/archive/2006/speeches/page43.aspx)

[42] Nina Shea, "Saudi Reform Pledge Publicly Distributed in July 2006 by U.S. State Department Officials," *Ten Years On: Saudi Arabia's Textbooks Still Promote Religious Violence* (Hudson Institute, 2011), page 47.
(https://www.hudson.org/content/researchattachments/attachment/931/sauditextbooks2011final.pdf)

[43] Cited in David Andrew Weinberg, "Textbook Diplomacy: Why the State Department Shelved a Study on Incitement in Saudi Education Materials," *Foundation for Defense of Democracies*, March 2014, page 7.
(http://www.defenddemocracy.org/content/uploads/documents/Textbook_Diplomacy.pdf)

[44] U.S. Department of State, "Saudi Arabia," *2009 Country Reports on Human Rights Practices*, March 11, 2010.
(https://www.state.gov/j/drl/rls/hrrpt/2009/nea/136079.htm)

[45] Quoted in David Andrew Weinberg, "Textbook Diplomacy: Why the State Department Shelved a Study on Incitement in Saudi Education Materials," *Foundation for Defense of Democracies*, March 2014, page 8.
(http://www.defenddemocracy.org/content/uploads/documents/Textbook_Diplomacy.pdf)

[46] U.S. Commission on International Religious Freedom, "Annual Report 2012," March 2012, page 167.
(http://www.uscirf.gov/sites/default/files/resources/Annual%20Report%20of%20USCIRF%202012(2).pdf)

David Andrew Weinberg   July 19, 2017

reforming the textbooks for grades one through nine had been fully completed by the end of 2012.[47] However, ICRD reported that even these textbooks still contained some deeply problematic passages. For example, an eighth-grade textbook that has supposedly been already fixed still *literally* taught hatred, admonishing students to hate non-believers, as well as calling for the execution of sorcerers.[48]

Other problematic passages noted by ICRD in these elementary and middle school books that were supposedly fixed included: passages that promoted or glorified "aggressive jihad," encouraged "extreme bias toward non-Muslims" and were "very harmful" for Saudi religious minorities, "gratuitous negative references to Jews and Christians," and "sweeping indictments" of them as polytheists.[49] According to Hannah Rosenthal, when she was serving as the State Department's Special Envoy to Monitor and Combat Anti-Semitism, a Saudi official asserted to her in 2011 that a passage calling Jews the spawn of monkeys or pigs was no longer in use,[50] even though it actually continued to be taught for at least several more years.[51]

If this is what qualifies as a thoroughly revised textbook in Saudi Arabia, then claims that this process may have finally been extended up through the twelfth grade require renewed scrutiny, not the termination of it.

The Saudis also missed several deadlines after that. In 2011, the kingdom's deputy education minister reportedly told the U.S. Commission on International Religious Freedom that the books would be completely revised by 2013.[52] The Commission then reported in 2013 that Saudi officials told them that the process of revising these books, including for grades 10 through 12, would be completed by 2014.[53]

---

[47] U.S. Department of State, "Saudi Arabia," *2012 International Religious Freedom Report*, May 20, 2013, page 14. (https://www.state.gov/documents/organization/208622.pdf)

[48] "The State of Tolerance in the Curriculum of the Kingdom of Saudi Arabia," *International Center for Religion and Diplomacy*, 2012, page 21. (https://www.nytimes.com/interactive/2016/08/17/international-home/document-state-dept-study-on-saudi-textbooks.html)

[49] "The State of Tolerance in the Curriculum of the Kingdom of Saudi Arabia," *International Center for Religion and Diplomacy*, 2012, pages 21-25. (https://www.nytimes.com/interactive/2016/08/17/international-home/document-state-dept-study-on-saudi-textbooks.html)

[50] Ron Kampeas, "U.S. State Dept. to Study Saudi Texts," *Jewish Telegraphic Agency*, July 7, 2011. (http://www.jta.org/2011/07/07/news-opinion/united-states/u-s-state-dept-to-study-saudi-texts)

[51] Nina Shea, *Ten Years On: Saudi Arabia's Textbooks Still Promote Religious Violence* (Hudson Institute, 2011), page 15. (https://www.hudson.org/content/researchattachments/attachment/931/sauditextbooks2011final.pdf); "The State of Tolerance in the Curriculum of the Kingdom of Saudi Arabia," *International Center for Religion and Diplomacy*, 2012, page 40. (https://www.nytimes.com/interactive/2016/08/17/international-home/document-state-dept-study-on-saudi-textbooks.html); Margherita Stancati and Ahmed Al Omran, "Saudis Ready Digital Push to Get Islamic Extremism out of Schools: Textbooks were Criticized after 9/11 for Tendentious Content Pitting Muslims against Other Religions," *The Wall Street Journal*, February 15, 2017. (https://www.wsj.com/articles/saudis-ready-digital-push-to-get-islamic-extremism-out-of-schools-1487154603)

[52] U.S. Commission on International Religious Freedom, "Annual Report 2012," March 2012, page 167. (http://www.uscirf.gov/sites/default/files/resources/Annual%20Report%20of%20USCIRF%202012(2).pdf); Nina Shea, *Ten Years On: Saudi Arabia's Textbooks Still Promote Religious Violence* (Hudson Institute, 2011), page 12. (https://www.hudson.org/content/researchattachments/attachment/931/sauditextbooks2011final.pdf);

[53] U.S. Commission on International Religious Freedom, "Annual Report 2013," April 2013, page 136. (http://www.uscirf.gov/sites/default/files/resources/2013%20USCIRF%20Annual%20Report%20(2).pdf)

                                                    July 19, 2017

In February 2017, Saudi Arabia's education minister said that the kingdom had made strides in reforming its education system to meet the nation's needs and "get rid of extremism," but that "I think we still have to do a lot in that direction."[54] According to the *Wall Street Journal*, he anticipated a "broader curriculum overhaul" after completing a project to shift Saudi classrooms from using printed materials to electronic tablets, which was expected to take up to three years.[55]

IV. Have the Books Improved at All?

Absolutely, and this is important to recognize while at the same time not treating it as an excuse to avoid raising the issue urgently with Riyadh.

Some particularly egregious passages evident in past editions have not been spotted in the textbooks of late. For example, I found the *Protocols of the Elders of Zion*, a notorious anti-Semitic hoax,[56] being taught in Saudi textbooks as recently as 2015-2016 but have not yet seen it in those books I have been able to examine for 2016-2017. Whereas previous Saudi books frequently instructed students to "hate" non-believers,[57] I have seen less of this language in the latest edition. More often, such language is instead framed somewhat less harshly, as a directive not to befriend non-believers because it says they are enemies of Muslims and Allah. As noted above, encouragements of violence are still in the curriculum as well, but they are also less common.

Simultaneously, some passages recommending tolerance have been added to the curriculum over the last sixteen years. Examples noted this year by the *Wall Street Journal* included: "terrorism is a form of corruption that God has forbidden" and terrorism "cannot be considered a form of Islamic jihad," "the prayer of the oppressed, whether from a Muslim or a non-Muslim, is answered," and "Islam is eager to strengthen bonds of love and brotherhood."[58]

The ICRD's 2012 report on Saudi textbooks also found a number of positive passages that had been added to the curriculum, even though extensive incitement still remained. Positive examples cited by ICRD included: two passages describing some or all "people of the book" (meaning Christians, Jews, and Muslims) as "believers," a passage about human rights under Islam that declares "an Arab has no superiority over a non-Arab," a passage that says the Quran "commands us to treat parents well and with respect, regardless of whether they are Muslims or non-Muslims,"

---

[54] Margherita Stancati and Ahmed Al Omran, "Saudis Ready Digital Push to Get Islamic Extremism out of Schools: Textbooks were Criticized after 9/11 for Tendentious Content Pitting Muslims against Other Religions," *The Wall Street Journal*, February 15, 2017. (https://www.wsj.com/articles/saudis-ready-digital-push-to-get-islamic-extremism-out-of-schools-1487154603)

[55] Margherita Stancati and Ahmed Al Omran, "Saudis Ready Digital Push to Get Islamic Extremism out of Schools: Textbooks were Criticized after 9/11 for Tendentious Content Pitting Muslims against Other Religions," *The Wall Street Journal*, February 15, 2017. (https://www.wsj.com/articles/saudis-ready-digital-push-to-get-islamic-extremism-out-of-schools-1487154603)

[56] United States Holocaust Memorial Museum, "Protocols of the Elders of Zion," *Holocaust Encyclopedia*, accessed July 16, 2017. (https://www.ushmm.org/wlc/en/article.php?ModuleId=10007058)

[57] U.S. Department of State, "Saudi Arabia," *2011 International Religious Freedom Report*, July 30, 2012, p. 13. (https://www.state.gov/documents/organization/193117.pdf)

[58] Slides associated with Margherita Stancati and Ahmed Al Omran, "Saudis Ready Digital Push to Get Islamic Extremism out of Schools: Textbooks were Criticized after 9/11 for Tendentious Content Pitting Muslims against Other Religions," *The Wall Street Journal*, February 15, 2017. (https://www.wsj.com/articles/saudis-ready-digital-push-to-get-islamic-extremism-out-of-schools-1487154603)

                                                              July 19, 2017

and a passage specifying that "treating a peaceful *kafer* [infidel or non-believer] kindly ... is not considered to be forbidden loyalty."[59]

Saudi Arabia has also spent lavishly on teacher training and expanded the teaching of STEM subjects (science, technology, engineering, and math), for which it receives frequent U.S. praise.[60] But critics rightly point out that these projects often are used as a distraction from the main problem for U.S. interests: the continued re-publication of incitement year after year by a U.S. ally in its public school curriculum.[61]

V. Why U.S. Policy Needs to Change

The default American approach to this issue is basically to wait and see, what former State Department official Thomas Farr decried as "no particular sense of urgency" back in 2008. And although working-level bureaucrats sporadically try to look at this issue, they lack the resources, authorization, and mandate to do so in-depth and regularly enough to have enough impact. They also lack the support necessary from American leaders, who almost never raise the books in a serious, detailed, and sustained manner with their Saudi counterparts.

This approach is a formula for failure.

Over a decade-and-a-half has passed since 9/11, and yet millions of Saudi school children have continued to be subjected to these inhumane lessons. Undoubtedly, such incitement has made America and our allies less secure, making it easier for the terrorist groups that we are fighting – and that target the kingdom itself – to attract potential new recruits.

Saudi Arabia has not been given a sufficient incentive to undertake the necessary changes to its textbooks in an urgent enough timeframe. Failing to launch a concerted effort to address Saudi textbooks now would also mean missing a moment of unusual U.S. leverage with Riyadh.

The Saudi leadership is so eager to see the Trump team follow through on its tough rhetoric regarding Iran that they are willing to go to great lengths to stay in America's good graces. Furthermore, the kingdom's campaign to mobilize international pressure against Qatar's reckless policies means that Saudi Arabia now has extra motivation to respond to public or private concerns about its own record.

VI. Common Counterarguments

I have encountered several main counterarguments to the perspective that America should be pressing Riyadh more actively to eliminate incitement from its textbooks.

---

[59] "The State of Tolerance in the Curriculum of the Kingdom of Saudi Arabia," *International Center for Religion and Diplomacy*, 2012, pages 93-96. (https://www.nytimes.com/interactive/2016/08/17/international-home/document-state-dept-study-on-saudi-textbooks.html)

[60] Royal Saudi Embassy in Washington, DC, "Saudi Arabia and Counterterrorism," April 2017, page 49. (https://www.saudiembassy.net/sites/default/files/White%20Paper_Counterterrorism_April2017_0_0.pdf)

[61] David Andrew Weinberg, "Textbook Diplomacy: Why the State Department Shelved a Study on Incitement in Saudi Education Materials," *Foundation for Defense of Democracies*, March 2014, pages 7-8. (http://www.defenddemocracy.org/content/uploads/documents/Textbook_Diplomacy.pdf)

David Andrew Weinberg

The most reasonable one – with which I still do not agree – is that making a priority out of the textbooks issue cannot be done without sacrificing other important American interests that pertain to the Saudis. Policy-makers can and should debate how best to raise this issue without jettisoning other critical priorities with Riyadh.

But more often, the counterarguments that I encounter assert something else: that America bringing up the books would either be unfair or hurt reformers more that it would help. I find these arguments unpersuasive for the following reasons.

First, some argue that it would be hypocritical for the United States, which was founded on religious liberty, to tell another nation what to believe. But raising this issue is not the same thing as dictating to Saudi citizens what private beliefs they should hold. It is beseeching a U.S.-allied government to stop publishing passages in state documents that threaten the religious liberties and right to life of others, especially when Saudi officials themselves have acknowledged that some passages in their curriculum do encourage extremism or sow discord.[62]

Others argue that outside pressure makes it harder for Saudi Arabia to reform its textbooks because it encourages hardliners to dig in their heels. Conservatives and preachers undoubtedly care about this issue; but sadly, addressing the incitement in textbooks has never been a top priority for the kingdom's rulers. Otherwise, they should have been able to resolve the problem by now without external engagement, as they repeatedly assured us would happen.

Instead, the most explicit Saudi government commitment to address this issue occurred in 2006, just two weeks after Nina Shea's report on Saudi textbooks revealed that kingdom's claims to have already resolved the issue of incitement in its textbooks were inaccurate.[63] Whereas Saudi Shiites I encounter – the victims of such incitement – tend to argue for U.S. pressure over the textbooks issue,[64] it is usually Sunnis close to the regime or Americans focused on eliciting Saudi cooperation on other issues – who argue that pressuring the Saudis would hurt rather than help Saudi textbook reform.

Another frequent counterargument is the claim that observant Muslim rulers like the Saudis are simply religiously unable to remove holy directives from state texts. But there are many Muslim-majority nations with Muslim rulers that choose not to write such egregious forms of incitement in their state curriculum. There is no religious stricture unambiguously mandating that the textbook of a Muslim state must emphasize particular lines or lessons from scripture. And there are plenty of lines from which to draw in the Quran and its commentaries that favor coexistence, compassion,

---

[62] Abdallah Yahya al-Mouallimi, "الدالوة .. رمز الوحدة الوطنية," *al-Madina* (Saudi Arabia), November 10. 2014. (http://www.al-madina.com/article/341901/); Margherita Stancati and Ahmed Al Omran, "Saudis Ready Digital Push to Get Islamic Extremism out of Schools: Textbooks were Criticized after 9/11 for Tendentious Content Pitting Muslims against Other Religions," *The Wall Street Journal*, February 15, 2017. (https://www.wsj.com/articles/saudis-ready-digital-push-to-get-islamic-extremism-out-of-schools-1487154603)
[63] David Andrew Weinberg, "Textbook Diplomacy: Why the State Department Shelved a Study on Incitement in Saudi Education Materials," *Foundation for Defense of Democracies*, March 2014, pages 6 and 9. (http://www.defenddemocracy.org/content/uploads/documents/Textbook_Diplomacy.pdf)
[64] See also Thomas F. Farr, *World of Faith and Freedom: Why International Religious Liberty is Vital to American National Security* (Oxford, 2008), page 238.

David Andrew Weinberg   July 19, 2017

tolerance, and peace. For example, King Salman and his predecessor Abdullah have both admirably emphasized the Quranic dictum that "there is no compulsion in religion."[65] It has also been persuasively argued by ICRD that on balance, the Quran is considerably less negative toward Christians and Jews that the Saudi curriculum.[66] Further, some of the lessons in these books – such as those calling for killing people for acts considered immoral – are even more extreme than Saudi policy, since they fail to make clear that such killing must only be conducted by the state and that the bar for such executions should be prohibitively high.

Finally, some argue that Saudi rulers are simply incapable of moving textbook reform forward more quickly because they are abjectly dependent upon the kingdom's conservative clerical establishment. And while Saudi rulers do look to senior clerics for regime support, they are also capable of making textbook reform a greater relative priority among other culturally contentious topics that the Saudi government is seeking to advance – over, say, hosting the first Saudi "Comic Con" convention last year and working to open a new Six Flags amusement park.[67] The clerical establishment was wary of these moves, but the government pushed forward successfully nonetheless. Indeed, Saudi rulers have historically been able to implement important reforms despite reluctance from the clergy when it suits the needs of the state, such as with the abolition of slavery, the introduction of television, the hosting American troops during the first Gulf War, and passing limitations on the austere religious police last year.

VII. Policy Recommendations

More than fifteen years after 9/11, it is unfortunate that we still need to be here today to discuss continued religious incitement in the government-published textbooks of a pivotal American ally. But the good news is there is plenty that members of Congress can do to make a difference if they choose to act.

1. Require Timely, Detailed, and Annual U.S. Public Reviews

In its most recent annual report, the U.S. Commission on International Religious Freedom called for the executive branch to "undertake and make public an annual assessment of the relevant Ministry of Education religious textbooks to determine if passages that teach religious intolerance have been removed."[68] Congress should pass legislation requiring the executive branch to do exactly that, and should allocate appropriate funding to do so. Legislation of this sort should require such a public reporting to be as detailed as possible, including full quotations of all passages that could be seen as encouraging violence or being derogatory toward adherents of other religions. It should require that the U.S. government complete its review within 90 days from the start of the new Saudi school year each September to ensure its results are valid long enough that

---

[65] U.S. Department of State, *Saudi Arabia 2013 Report on International Religious Freedom,* July 28, 2014, page 16. (https://www.state.gov/documents/organization/222523.pdf)

[66] "The State of Tolerance in the Curriculum of the Kingdom of Saudi Arabia," *International Center for Religion and Diplomacy,* 2012, pages 83-91. (https://www.nytimes.com/interactive/2016/08/17/international-home/document-state-dept-study-on-saudi-textbooks.html)

[67] Katie Paul and William Maclean, "Saudi Entertainment Chief Sees Cinemas Returning, Eventually," *Reuters,* April 27, 2017. (http://www.reuters.com/article/us-saudi-entertainment-idUSKBN17T2WP)

[68] U.S. Commission on International Religious Freedom, "2017 Annual Report," April 2017, page 76. (http://www.uscirf.gov/sites/default/files/2017.USCIRFAnnualReport.pdf)

David Andrew Weinberg   July 19, 2017

U.S. officials can engage extensively with Riyadh while books are still current and before drafting of the next edition is finalized. If Saudi officials do not make the books available in time for such an assessment, the U.S. should revisit Saudi Arabia's longstanding waiver under the International Religious Freedom Act, first granted in 2006 in part based on assurances that its textbooks would be fully revised long ago.[69] Legislation should also require that copies of these books be made available in the Library of Congress for private researchers and Congressional staff.

2. Require an Assessment of Saudi Exportation of Incitement

Direct the U.S. intelligence community to monitor for instances in which Saudi Arabia's government-backed exportation of religious messages involves propagating incitement, and allocate appropriate resources for it to do so. Mandate one-time or ongoing governmental reporting to Congress on the matter, primarily in an unclassified format and with a classified annex if appropriate, but only to the extent necessary to protect sources and methods.

3. Insist on the Nomination of Relevant U.S. Envoys

Roughly half a year has passed, and yet at the time of writing this, the new U.S. administration still has not picked a nominee for ambassador to Saudi Arabia. It also has not nominated an ambassador-at-large for international religious freedom, a special representative to Muslim communities, a special envoy to monitor and combat anti-Semitism, or a special envoy to promote religious freedom of religious minorities in the Near East and South and Central Asia with the rank of ambassador, even though three of these four positions are mandated by act of Congress.[70] Members of Congress should raise this with the administration in public and in private until nominees for all five positions have been named.

4. Call on Saudi Arabia to Replace Old Textbooks Overseas

In its most recent annual report, the U.S. Commission on International Religious Freedom called on the U.S. to "press the Saudi government to denounce publicly the continued use around the world of older versions of Saudi textbooks and other materials that promote hatred and intolerance, and to make every attempt to retrieve, or buy back, previously distributed materials that contain intolerance."[71] Members of Congress should add their voice to this call, both in public and in private, and use letters or legislation to urge the administration to do so as well.

5. Encourage Rebooting the U.S.-Saudi Strategic Dialogue

The George W. Bush administration launched an annual strategic dialogue with Saudi Arabia in 2005 to ensure that issues of concern to either side would get a full hearing even when top leaders

---

[69] U.S. Department of State, Press Release, "Ambassador at Large for International Religious Freedom Briefs Congress on U.S.-Saudi Discussions on Religious Practice and Tolerance," July 19, 2006. (https://2001-2009.state.gov/r/pa/prs/ps/2006/69197.htm)

[70] "Tracking How Many Key Positions Trump Has Filled So Far," *The Washington Post*, updated July 14, 2017, accessed July 16, 2017. (https://www.washingtonpost.com/graphics/politics/trump-administration-appointee-tracker/database/)

[71] U.S. Commission on International Religious Freedom, "2017 Annual Report," April 2017, page 76. (http://www.uscirf.gov/sites/default/files/2017.USCIRFAnnualReport.pdf)

are preoccupied with other matters. That dialogue lapsed during the Obama administration, but it should be restarted. The new crown prince of Saudi Arabia is said to support such an idea as well.[72] One of the working groups should be expressly designed to address the U.S. concerns about incitement (in textbooks and other venues) as well as human rights, while also giving Saudi Arabia an opportunity to advocate for the rights and dignity of Muslims in America.

6. Raise Saudi Textbooks, Publicly and Privately, as a Priority Issue

Members of Congress should raise the issue of incitement in Saudi textbooks both privately and publicly. They should encourage the president and secretary of state to address it as well, and urge President Trump to issue a formal directive to cabinet members and U.S. agencies to make the issue a priority in U.S.-Saudi relations.

While in Saudi Arabia this May, President Trump participated in the inauguration of a Global Center for Combating Extremist Ideology, which he predicted "will make history."[73] Reflecting on his visit to the kingdom several weeks later, he urged all nations to "stop teaching people to kill other people. Stop filling their minds with hate and intolerance."[74] Trump said he would not "name other countries" besides Qatar,[75] but without addressing the issue of Saudi textbooks more directly, our Saudi allies will simply continue doing what they have been doing: reprinting incitement year after year while whittling away at the edges. In the meantime, these deeply problematic books will be delivered to another generation of school children.

---

[72] Bilal Y. Saab, "Can Mohamed bin Salman Reshape Saudi Arabia? The Treacherous Path to Reform," *Foreign Affairs*, January 5, 2017. (https://www.foreignaffairs.com/articles/saudi-arabia/2017-01-05/can-mohamed-bin-salman-reshape-saudi-arabia)

[73] White House, Press Release, "President Trump's Speech to the Arab Islamic American Summit," May 21, 2017. (https://www.whitehouse.gov/the-press-office/2017/05/21/president-trumps-speech-arab-islamic-american-summit)

[74] White House, Press Release, "Remarks by President Trump and President Iohannis of Romania in a Joint Press Conference," June 9, 2017. (https://www.whitehouse.gov/the-press-office/2017/06/09/remarks-president-trump-and-president-iohannis-romania-joint-press)

[75] White House, Press Release, "Remarks by President Trump and President Iohannis of Romania in a Joint Press Conference," June 9, 2017. (https://www.whitehouse.gov/the-press-office/2017/06/09/remarks-president-trump-and-president-iohannis-romania-joint-press)

Mr. POE. Thank you, Dr. Weinberg.

The Chair will now recognize Congressman Wolf.

STATEMENT OF THE HONORABLE FRANK WOLF, DISTINGUISHED SENIOR FELLOW, 21ST CENTURY WILBERFORCE INITIATIVE (FORMER U.S. REPRESENTATIVE)

Mr. WOLF. Thank you, Mr. Chairman and members of the committee.

The issue of Saudi educational curriculum as a means of promoting intolerance and inspiring terrorism is not a new one. This topic hit close to home in 2003, when Ahmed Omar Abu Ali was arrested while in class at the Islamic University of Medina for an attempted plot to assassinate President Bush. Before attending the University of Medina, Mr. Abu Ali attended and was a valedictorian at a high school which was located here in northern Virginia, the Islamic Saudi Academy. Mr. Abu Ali was ultimately sentenced to life in prison and is currently serving out his sentence in a supermax in Colorado.

The reason I would like to highlight this particular case in particular is due to the fact that concerns were raised regarding the educational material being used by the Islamic Saudi Academy over and over. Not only was the school funded by the Saudi Arabian Embassy, which meant it fell under the Saudi Ministry of Education, but the Saudi Ambassador to Washington led the board of directors. He literally led the school.

In 2007 when asked by the United States Commission on International Religious Freedom to make textbooks publicly available, the school refused to comply. We got copies from a professor that gave us one on the side. One letter from USCIRF on the issue stated, "Based on past documentation, significant concerns remain about whether the Saudi textbooks used at the ISA Academy explicitly . . . hate, intolerance and human rights violations, and in some cases violence, which may adversely affect the interests of the United States."

In 2008, I wrote Secretary Rice on five different occasions regarding the concerns held by the Commission regarding the content of the textbooks. At that time I requested a meeting be convened between relevant State Department officials, USCIRF representatives, and expert analysts commissioned by USCIRF to translate the textbooks in order to determine what was being taught by the Academy. Such meeting never took place.

Generally, the State Department has been weak on this issue in both Republican and in Democratic administrations.

During this time, USCIRF was finally able to obtain copies of some of the textbooks being used by the Islamic Saudi Academy. After a thorough analysis, the Commission concluded that the textbooks contained very troubling passages that did not conform to international human rights standards, including vilification of those who adhere to Christianity, Judaism, Baha'i'ism, Ahmadism, and Shia Islam and others. I have submitted for the record some of those statements.

And in 2009 I sent a letter, again, to Secretary of State Clinton, urging the State Department monitor and report on the textbooks published by the Saudi Government. In that letter I acknowledged,

"To date, we have had only vague assurances on the part of the State Department and the school that the curriculum has been reformed. But these assurances are insufficient, particularly when they are utterly at odds with USCIRF's findings, and may be indicative of wider problems, namely, the status of Saudi commitments made in 2006 to conduct a comprehensive revision of textbooks and educational curricula to weed out . . ."

While it is impossible to say that Mr. Abu Ali was directly radicalized by the textbooks used at the Islamic Saudi Academy, the use of the books that promote religious discrimination and the justification of violence toward non-believers cannot be tolerated, certainly not in Fairfax County, not in Virginia, not in America, but quite frankly, anywhere around the world.

Consider that if this is the academy's curriculum in the United States, just imagine how prolific the problem has been across Saudi-affiliated academies, funded programs in other countries around the world, especially in some countries in the Middle East.

While the Ahmed Omar Abu Ali case is now almost a decade old, Saudi Arabia has continued to promote and export radical Wahhabism. In the wake of the Orlando shooting just last year, Democratic Presidential nominee Hillary Clinton stated, "It is long past the time for the Saudis, the Qataris and the Kuwaitis and others to stop their citizens from funding extremist organizations. And they should stop," she said, "supporting radical schools and mosques around the world that have set too many young people on the path toward extremism."

And, unfortunately, by funding top American university research centers, the Saudi Government has been able to minimize voices of those in academia who you would have thought otherwise would have had the best means for researching the effects of radical Wahhabism.

While there are many concerns regarding the influence of Saudi Arabia, more specifically radical Wahhabism, on countries around the world, it would be remiss not to acknowledge that very recently some small improvements have been made to the educational material. In the latest report by USCIRF they said, "In February 2017 Saudi officials stated that the final stage of revisions to high school texts was underway. During its visit, USCIRF obtained some textbooks currently in use and found some intolerant content remained in high school texts, though at a reduced level."

They go on to explain while there has been progress in terms, there is still concern that some of the teachers may be promoting a more radicalized version of Islam.

Some recommendations: One, the USCIRF has some very good recommendations. Undertake and make public and annual assessment.

I believe you have to put this in the legislation. If you just let the State Department or the American Embassy in Saudi Arabia, they will always find a reason not to do it. So I think it needs to be mandated that the relevant Ministry of Education textbooks determine the passages that teach religious intolerance have been removed.

Secondly, press the Saudi Government to denounce publicly the continued use around the world of older versions of Saudi textbooks and other materials that promote hatred and intolerance. And make every attempt to retrieve and buy back previously distributed textbooks that contain intolerance.

You know, even in America's schools sometimes you're in a class there will be a textbook that is 10, 15 years old. These are still in schools around, around the world.

And keep in mind, lastly, the Saudis funded almost all of the madrasas that were up on the Afghan-Pakistan border that helped lead to what took place in the Taliban. Mullah Omar, the head of the Taliban, was a graduate of a Saudi-funded academy. The issue needs more work.

And I want to thank the subcommittee and the members because I kind of thought for a while this issue was kind of forgotten about. Mandate it and put it in. If you take the pressure off the Saudis they will slip back in and this will come in. You keep the pressure on and you can make a tremendous difference.

I thank you for the hearing.

[The prepared statement of Mr. Wolf follows:]

Committee on Foreign Affairs
Subcommittee on Terrorism, Nonproliferation, and Trade
"Saudi Arabia's Troubling Educational Curriculum"
Hon. Frank Wolf- Written Testimony
July 19, 2017

Mr. Chairman, Members of the Committee, thank you for having this hearing regarding concerns about Saudi Arabia's educational curriculum and the rise of radicalization. I have shared these same concerns for many years when I served in the House and since joining the Wilberforce Initiative in 2015, and it is my hope that the U.S. government will continue to monitor and assess the educational materials that the government of Saudi Arabia publishes in order to ensure that they do not incite further violence, hatred and radicalism in the United States as well as abroad. We should also consider solutions that ensure other countries that may produce similar intolerant and extreme content is addressed.

The issue of Saudi Arabia's educational curriculum as a means of promoting intolerance and inspiring terrorism is not a new one. This topic hit close to home in 2003, when Ahmed Omar Abu Ali was arrested while in class at the Islamic University of Medina, for an attempted plot to assassinate President Bush. Before attending university in Medina, Mr. Abu Ali attended and was the valedictorian at a high school which was located here in northern Virginia, the Islamic Saudi Academy. Mr. Abu Ali was ultimately sentenced to life in prison and is currently serving out his sentence in the supermax in Colorado.

The reason I would like to highlight this particular case in particular is due to the fact that concerns were then raised regarding the educational material being used by the Islamic Saudi Academy. Not only was the school funded by the Saudi Arabian Embassy, which meant it fell under the Saudi ministry of education, but the Saudi Ambassador to Washington led the Board of Directors for the school.

In 2007, when asked by the United States Commission on International Religious Freedom to make the textbooks publicly available, the school refused to comply. One letter from USCIRF on the issue stated, "Based on past documentation, significant concerns remain about whether the Saudi textbooks used at the ISA explicitly promote hate, intolerance and human rights violations, and in some cases violence, which may adversely affect the interests of the United States."

In 2008, I wrote then Secretary of State Condoleezza Rice on five separate occasions regarding the concerns held by the United States Commission on International Religious Freedom regarding the content of the textbooks being used by the Islamic Saudi Academy. At that time I requested that a meeting be convened between relevant State Department officials, USCIRF representatives and expert analysts commissioned by USCIRF to translate the textbooks in order to determine what was being taught by the ISA. Such a meeting never took place.

During this time, USCIRF was finally able to obtain copies of some of the textbooks being used by the Islamic Saudi Academy. After a thorough analysis, the Commission concluded that the textbooks contained some very troubling passages that did not conform to international human rights standards- including the vilification of those who adhere to Christianity, Judaism, Baha"ism, Ahmadism, Shia Islam and others. I have submitted for the record a letter that the Commission released on June 11, 2008 which contains examples of some of the statements made in the textbooks.

Again, in 2009, I sent a letter to then Secretary of State Hillary Clinton, urging that the State Department monitor and report on the textbooks published by the Saudi government. In that letter, I acknowledged that, "To date, we have only had vague assurances on the part of the State Department and the school that the curriculum has been reformed. But these assurances are insufficient, particularly when they are utterly at odds with USCIRF's findings, and may be indicative of a wider problem- namely the status of Saudi commitments made in 2006 to conduct 'a comprehensive revision of textbooks and educational curricula to weed out disparaging remarks.'"

While it is impossible to say whether Mr. Abu Ali was directly radicalized by the textbooks used at the Islamic Saudi Academy, the use of books that promote religious discrimination and the justification of violence toward non-believers cannot be tolerated. Consider that if this is the Academy's curriculum in the United States, just imagine how prolific this problem has been across Saudi-affiliated academies and funded programs in other countries around the world, especially in countries in the Middle East, that are struggling with radicalization and terrorism.

While the Ahmed Omar Abu Ali case is now almost a decade old, Saudi Arabia has continued to promote and export radical Wahhabism. In the wake of the Orlando shooting just last year, Democratic Presidential nominee, Hillary Clinton, stated, "It is long past time for the Saudis, the Qataris and the Kuwaitis and others to stop their citizens from funding extremist organization. And they should stop supporting radical schools and mosques around the world that have set too many young people on a path towards extremism."

By funding top American university research centers, the Saudi government has been able to minimize the voices of those in academia who would otherwise have the best means of researching the effects of radical Wahhabism. In other countries, such as Bosnia, Albania, Kosovo and Indonesia they have continued to promote radicalism. In an op-ed by Nicholas Kristoff entitled, "The Terrorists the Saudis Cultivate in Peaceful Countries," he states, "Kosovo and Albania have been models of religious moderation and tolerance...Yet Saudi Arabia and other Gulf countries poured money into the new nation over the last 17 years and nurtured religious extremism in a land where originally there was little." In an article that appeared in the New York Times last year, entitled, "Saudis and Extremism: 'Both the Arsonists and the Firefighters,'" the author details that since the mid-60's, "in non-Muslim-majority countries alone, Saudi Arabia would build 1,359 mosques, 210 Islamic centers, 202 colleges and 2,000 schools. Saudi money helped finance 16 American mosques; four in Canada; and others in London, Madrid, Brussels and Geneva, according to a report in an official Saudi weekly, Ain al-Yaqeen. The total spending including supplying or training imams and teachers, was 'many billions' of Saudi riyals."

While there are many concerns regarding the influence of Saudi Arabia, and more specifically radical Wahhabism, on countries around the world, it would be remiss to not acknowledge that very recently, some improvements have been made to their educational material. In the latest report by the United States Commission on International Religious Freedom it states, "In February 2017, Saudi officials stated that the final stage of revisions to high school textbooks was underway…During its visit, USCIRF obtained some textbooks currently in use and found some intolerant content remained in high school texts, though at a much-reduced level." They go on to explain that while there has been progress in terms of the textbooks, there is still a concern that some of the teachers may be promoting a more radicalized version of Islam. However, the Ministry of Education has undertaken an initiative through which teachers are encouraged to participate in teacher training in both Europe and the U.S.

There are certainly many improvements that must be made, but in closing I would like to echo the recommendations set forward by USCIRF that the United States government 1) Undertake and make public an annual assessment of the relevant Ministry of Education religious textbooks to determine if passages that teach religious intolerance have been removed and 2) Press the Saudi government to denounce publicly the continued use around the world of older versions of Saudi textbooks and other materials that promote hatred and intolerance, and to make every attempt to retrieve, or buy back, previously distributed materials that contain intolerance.

Thank you.

Mr. POE. Thank you, Congressman Wolf.

Dr. Johnston.

STATEMENT OF DOUGLAS JOHNSTON, PH.D., PRESIDENT EMERITUS, INTERNATIONAL CENTER FOR RELIGION AND DIPLOMACY

Mr. JOHNSTON. Yes, Mr. Chairman, I would like to thank you for the honor of presenting to your committee some of the work our center has been doing to try to help facilitate educational reform in the Kingdom of Saudi Arabia. We have a written testimony that covers that comprehensively. I will just touch on some of the highlights.

Before I do, though, I would like to just take 1 second to honor the other witnesses here. Each is a champion of human rights and religious freedom in their own right, and it is an honor to be with them.

Our task, which I consider complementary to their own, has been to take action to address the problem. And in 2011, we received a grant from the State Department to develop recommendations that would help facilitate reform efforts that were already underway in the Kingdom. Toward this end, we assessed all the textbooks for discriminatory content. And we also tried to determine global dispersion of those textbooks.

It was a—from the start our approach was one of seeking to be balanced, giving them credit for whatever progress had been made, not only in that but in their deradicalization program, but to be very unsparing in our detail of what yet remained to be done. And there we completed a report, very comprehensive, included 99 textbooks. I could go into great length on that, but just suffice it to say that this report is just replete with examples of the kinds of problems that have been cited here with the other witnesses.

There is, at that point in time, this is 2011, sprinkled throughout you would find direct license given for violent behavior toward others who do not subscribe to that similar brand of Islam. You would also find direct license for such things as desecrating the tombs of the Sufi saints in Timbuktu, which the extremists did before the French kicked them out. So, lots of problems.

There were not only problems in the textbooks as a whole, but even in the six grades that had already been thoroughly revised we did find problems.

So, one of the things I would just point out, though, in terms of looking at these things, I think it is important to try to avoid using a western lens as we do so. By that I mean what we try to do is hold their feet to the fire by comparing what is in those textbooks to what is in the Holy Quran with respect to that same subject area, what is in the Cairo Declaration of Human Rights in Islam with respect to that. In all cases, the Saudi textbooks were much more conservative than the sources I just mentioned.

So, that is, that is a very important piece is just understanding exactly where, how much freedom the Government of Saudi Arabia has to really maneuver. There are so many wild cards in the mix. There are charities through which textbooks are distributed. There are maverick members of the royal family. There are deep-pocketed

41

Saudis who are not members of the royal family. Lots of people with lots of agendas.

And one of the things that is also a bit of a constraint is the fact that the original pact between the monarchy and the Salafi Ulema called for education belongs to the religious establishment. So one of the things that the Saudis were having to do is to finesse that aspect, that obligation. They also need to worry about the credibility that they maintain within Islam itself as custodian of the two holiest sites. So this is, this is not to forgive any of the textbook content, this is to just explain why sometimes it may take a little bit longer than we would like.

We established a comprehensive baseline for future analysis. And we felt that the progress that the Saudis were making was credible enough that we should probably keep the report private, not release it to the public. Our concern was that western critics seizing upon the offensive passages that still remain might just shut down the whole process as a defensive backlash sets in and the conservatives move in. We have seen this time and again in different situations in the Islamic world.

So, we spent the next 3 years implementing some of the recommendations that we had come forward with.

Now, just to bring it right up to the present, we are in another month we are going to be starting a new effort to look at the textbooks of the high school grades which had not been revised the last time we looked at them. We are also going to take an in-depth look at three countries on how the Saudi educational materials are affecting the religious and social. What is that impact?

And I will say this, right now the Saudis claim to have just completed that process, reform process that started way back in 2007. And they realize, however, that they still have problems. Many of those have been mentioned here right now. And what they are planning to do is tackle it from two aspects.

One, is by 2020 to have developed a set of curriculum standards. They have never had curriculum standards before. And this is part of their national plan on educational reform which was articulated in 2014, $22 billion behind it. It is very serious money. That money has stayed protected even during their budget shortfalls. And by these curriculum standards they will then revise wholesale the content in all of the textbooks.

In the meantime, on a more urgent basis, they are going to be looking at the current revised textbooks and within—starting within 3 months they will start making changes on a priority basis. And they will have these completed, according to them, by the next school year, 2018 to 2019. And there is so much going on right now. They are going to—in 3 years they will have converted from textbooks to tablet computers. So there is a lot of change underway.

I believe that the commitment is real. And they certainly do understand the problem.

Thank you.

[The prepared statement of Mr. Johnston follows:]

Written Testimony
Dr. Douglas M. Johnston
President Emeritus, ICRD
before the
HFAC Subcommittee on Terrorism, Nonproliferation, and Trade
Hearing on
"Saudi Arabia's Troubling Educational Curriculum"
July 19, 2017

Mr. Chairman, thank you for the opportunity to share with your Subcommittee the work that the International Center for Religion & Diplomacy (ICRD) has been doing in support of the Kingdom of Saudi Arabia's efforts to facilitate educational reform. Before doing so, though, I would like to express my personal gratitude to the other witnesses who are testifying today for their highly effective efforts in identifying and calling to public attention the discriminatory content in the Kingdom's public school text books, which at its worst, can lead to extremist behavior or, short of that, to violations of religious freedom and other human rights. Our Center's mandate, which I consider complementary to their own, is to take corrective action to address the problem. Although we are by no means apologists for the Saudis, my purpose here today, as I understand it, is to report on the progress that is being made to address this issue.

Background

First, a bit of background. Following the attacks of 9-11 (in which 15 of the 19 hijackers were identified as Saudi nationals), the Kingdom faced strong external pressure to curb the spread of Wahhabism, especially through its public school textbooks, which had made their way across the globe and were inspiring terrorist groups like al-Qaeda. Two years later, after the Kingdom itself was rocked by a wave of al-Qaeda-led attacks, the first meaningful steps were taken toward educational reform (in concert with a strong de-radicalization program). However, it wasn't until 2007, soon after King Abdullah bin Abdulaziz al Saud ascended to the throne, that the Tatweer Education Reform project was launched to promote curriculum reform that would graduate "capable and open-minded" young Saudis.

ICRD Study

To support the Kingdom's educational reform efforts, the State Department awarded our Center a grant (Cooperative Agreement) in 2011 to develop recommendations for promoting educational reform in the Kingdom. Toward that end, we were to examine the discriminatory content in Saudi Arabia's public school textbooks, and to provide a basic overview of their global dispersion. In undertaking this assignment, we opted to take a balanced approach, giving full credit for any reforms that had already taken place (including those associated with the Kingdom's de-radicalization program), while being unsparing in our detail of what yet remained to be done.

This was consistent with a similar approach we had taken over an eight-year period in reforming the curriculums and pedagogy of more than 1,500 madrasas (religious schools) in the radical areas of Pakistan. Our success there was attributable to three factors: (1) sharing ownership in the change process (by conducting the project in such a way that the madrasa leaders felt it to be their reform effort and not something imposed from the outside); (2) appealing to their own heritage, not only of their schools, which in the Middle Ages were unrivaled as institutions of higher learning, but of Islam itself, which in its early years was responsible for a number of breakthroughs in the arts and sciences, including religious tolerance (at a time when Christianity was woefully intolerant); and (3) grounding all suggested change in Islamic principles (so they could feel they were becoming better Muslims in the process). We call this approach "organic suasion", i.e. promoting peace from within through respectful engagement.

As we began to understand the scope and seeming commitment of the Kingdom's educational reform effort, we concluded that the study should not be made public, lest Western critics use offensive passages that yet remained to chastise the Saudis and risk provoking a defensive backlash that could jeopardize the reform process. We felt that it would make more sense to help move things in a positive direction through quiet diplomacy rather than attempting to force change through further criticism.

In a similar vein, it is important to recognize certain sensitivities unique to the Saudi government, i.e. the need to maintain credibility with (1) its own religious establishment (under which "education" rightfully resides, according to the Kingdom's historic compact between the monarchy and the Salafist *Ulema*) and (2) Islam more generally (as Custodian of its two holiest sites).

Our review of the texts, which was the most comprehensive conducted to date, revealed that the Kingdom was making credible progress toward reform, but that much more was needed to complete the process. In short, the report provided an analysis of:

- The textbook changes that had taken place over the previous decade.

- The remaining areas of bias and intolerance that still existed in the textbooks, especially at the high school level.

- How the Wahhabist content of the textbooks compared to Quranic admonitions on the same topics (unfavorably, in almost every instance) and to the provisions of the Cairo Declaration on Human Rights in Islam (again almost universally unfavorable).

More specifically, the textbooks were examined for instances of religious intolerance, including misrepresentation of religious beliefs or identity, collective blame, pejorative historical narratives, and content that promoted or excused violence and aggression on the basis on religion.

As shown in the table below, the scope of the curriculum review covered a total of 99 textbooks from the national curriculum, of which the majority were from religious studies subjects, followed by history and social sciences, and finally, the language arts. We were also able to obtain textbooks on science, math, and technology, but they were not found to contain any objectionable content.

Level (Grade)	Total Books	Publication Year		Subject		
		2011-2012	1996-2010	Religious Studies	Social Science	Language Arts
Primary (1-6)	17	13	4	13	3	1
Intermediate (7-9)	27	11	16	22	5	0
High School (10-12)	55	35	20	34	15	6
	99	59	40	69	23	7

According to official statements from the Saudi Ministry of Education, the textbooks we examined included six grade levels from the primary and intermediate levels that had already undergone "thorough revisions." Of the primary and intermediate levels (grades 1-9), only three had not been revised, including grades three, six, and nine. It was reported that all of the secondary grade levels were undergoing revision, a process that was to be completed by 2013.

With notable exceptions, few examples of pejorative content were found in the revised textbooks from the primary grade levels. Although encouraging, these grades were not expected to contain much in the way of egregious content. Regarding the intermediate levels, the results of the revision process were inconsistent. Some intermediate level textbooks, such as the 8th grade text on *Hadith*, were almost completely free of intolerant content and even included positive messages such as the following:

> *"The prayer of the oppressed, be he Muslim or non-Muslim is answered and not rejected."*
> *Hadith, Grade Eight (Term II), p.57*

This progress, however, was not reflected in other eighth grade textbooks. For example, the *Monotheism* textbook contained a direct call for violence against "sorcerers", the *Jurisprudence* textbook advocated donating *zakat* (charitable) contributions to the *Mujahideen*, and the *Tafsir* textbook promoted violent jihad and contained anti-Semitic narratives.

Textbooks in the secondary grade levels, of which none had been revised, contained intolerant content as documented in earlier studies conducted by Nina Shea and others. Problematic material in these grade levels included direct and gratuitous criticism of the beliefs and practices of non-Muslims and non-Salafi Muslims, lessons that glorified an aggressive and violent concept of jihad; and inaccurate and pejorative historical narratives that cast Jews and Christians as eternal threats to Islam and Muslims everywhere.

Beyond the details, the study provided a comprehensive baseline for future analysis and offered helpful recommendations for immediate improvement.

In 2013, we began working to implement some of the study's key recommendations. Our first step during this phase was to brief a contingent of Saudi educational experts in Riyadh on the findings of the 2012 study. It was a highly successful encounter, and we proposed a follow-up meeting between American and Saudi scholars and education experts in the United States. With the approval of the Minister of Education and the King, the proposed meeting of American and Saudi educators took place at Georgetown University in November 2015.

The purpose of this meeting was to facilitate an atmosphere of shared problem-solving, while avoiding any specter of paternalism by bringing the two sides together as equals to address a problem they shared in common (i.e. the problem of bias and intolerance in national education systems). As backdrop for the discussion, we shared the results of a study that we (ICRD) had conducted on how a dozen other countries had dealt with similar problems. The meeting, which included officials from the Saudi Ministry of Education and from the U.S. Departments of State and Education, also addressed a number of key principles for advancing educational reform in the Muslim world.

After extensive discussion on various aspects of our respective educational systems, the head of the Saudi delegation gave a detailed presentation on his country's new National Strategy for Educational Reform, which was promulgated a year after ICRD's study first made its way to the Kingdom through diplomatic channels. This new strategy, funded at a level of $22 billion over four years, focuses on (1) curriculum development, (2) teacher training, (3) institutional capacity-building, and (4) development of 21st century skills, including those relating to cross-cultural communications. The ultimate goal is to enable Saudi youth to compete effectively in the globalized market place. Happily, this coincides with our own goals of instilling (1) a keen appreciation for diversity, (2) tolerance for other faiths and sects, (3) increased respect for human rights, and (4) a strong, ongoing commitment to critical thinking. Although the National Plan was undoubtedly driven more by national self-interest than by Western criticism, with continued effort, it seems likely that the inflammatory content in the public school textbooks will soon become a thing of the past.

The November meeting concluded with the Saudi and American delegations agreeing on a range of topics to be researched prior to a second meeting of the delegates in Riyadh, in May of 2016. Based on a later discussion of these topics at the Riyadh meeting, recommendations were developed for the consideration of both governments. In August of 2016, ICRD presented the recommendations for the Saudi government to Dr. Ahmed Aleisa, the Saudi Minister of Education, at a round-table discussion on educational reform, which he chaired in our

Washington office. Others in attendance included senior representatives from the U.S. Departments of State and Education.

Global Impact

To determine the degree to which Saudi texts have been dispersed throughout the Muslim and developing worlds, we based our findings on (1) extensive interviews and correspondence with experts from Africa, Eastern Europe, and Central and South Asia; (2) comprehensive desk research based on written reports, journal articles, and transcripts; and (3) field research in three countries. From what we could ascertain, the principal conduits through which most of these books have been distributed are Saudi Arabian humanitarian charities like the Muslim World League (MWL), the International Islamic Relief Organization (IIRO), the World Assembly (or Association) of Muslim Youth, the UK-based Al-Muqtada Organization, and the now-defunct Al-Haramain Fund (AHF). Most of the activity related to this distribution has taken the form of constructing new mosques, madrasas, and libraries throughout the developing world. Based on this research, we developed brief profiles of 35 countries where Saudi sources have been actively funding the construction and operation of religious schools.

The presence of Saudi textbooks and educational materials appeared to be most prevalent in Sub-Saharan Africa, where the Kingdom has been heavily involved in the construction and financing of mosques and madrasas since the 1960s. In countries like Burkina Faso, Mali, Nigeria, Somalia, and Tanzania, it was reported that Saudi funders maintained close oversight of the teacher training and educational materials used in the religious schools they had built. As might be expected, in countries like Kenya, with its more sophisticated restrictions on foreign financing of religious institutions, the Kingdom had noticeably less influence over education.

In Southeast Asia, Indonesia stood apart as a country where Saudi textbooks were widely distributed and used in Salafi madrasas in different parts of the country. However, as best we could determine, in those schools operated by Indonesia's (indeed, the world's) two largest Muslim organizations, Nahdlatul Ulema and Muhamadiyah (50 million and 40 million members respectively), Saudi textbooks were apparently not in use. In Central Asia and Eastern Europe, there was a significant effort by the Kingdom to gain influence following the collapse of the Soviet Union and the former Republic of Yugoslavia. With few exceptions, this effort has largely failed, owing to the tight control that most countries in these regions hold over educational curriculum.

Although direct observation by ICRD and its partnering organizations in Pakistan did not uncover the use of Saudi textbooks in the Ahle Hadith (Wahhabi) madrasas funded by Saudi Arabia, these schools were found to be using textbooks that contained similarly pejorative content, albeit of local origin.

While this study focused on the spread of Saudi textbooks, which clearly play a role in the advance of Wahhabist Salafism around the world, evidence suggests that the textbooks actually play a relatively minor role in comparison to the influence of the imams and teachers and, by direct extension, the training they receive.

The Road Ahead

Next month, we will take another look at the textbooks, this time assessing the content of the high school grades, which had not yet been revised at the time of our earlier look in 2012. We will also conduct an in-depth examination of the religious and social impact of Saudi educational materials in three countries of strategic consequence. The viability of conducting these studies in selected countries from the Middle East, Southeast Asia, and Western Europe is currently being assessed.

Although we have not examined Saudi textbook content in the last five years, the U.S. Commission on International Religious Freedom examined an incomplete set of textbooks several years ago and determined that the reform process was continuing. However, we have no reason to doubt the validity of any of the more recent examples of intolerant content cited by other scholars.

The pace of change in reforming the Kingdom's public school textbooks has been glacial at best. A process that was to have been completed in 2008, took until now to complete. Even with the additional time, though, significant problems remain. The Saudis are aware of these problems and are planning to address them on two levels. First, and consistent with the Crown Prince's 2030 Vision, a set of curriculum standards will be developed that will precipitate a wholesale revision of all textbook content. Toward this end, the first draft of a Curriculum Framework has been developed to provide a basis for crafting the standards. This process is scheduled to be completed in 2020, and it will represent the first time in the Kingdom's history that such standards have existed. Without curriculum standards that specify what students should learn and be able to do, it becomes exceedingly difficult to hold teachers and textbook authors accountable.

On a more urgent basis, the Ministry of Education will be assessing the revised textbooks for oppressive content and begin making changes on a real-time, priority basis, allegedly within the next three months. The Ministry's timetable calls for having this process completed in time for the 2018-2019 academic year.

As for the global impact of existing textbooks, in response to ICRD's earlier study on this subject, a request went out in May 2016 to all Saudi embassies around the world, urging them to retrieve any older textbooks that might be in use within their respective geographic areas and to replace them with the newer, revised editions. Extensive follow-up is taking place, and there has apparently been an encouraging response. An important caveat here is that the Saudi government doesn't know all of the locations in which its textbooks are being used, since it has not had total control of their distribution.

A Sobering Challenge

With a perfect storm descending on Saudi Arabia in the form of low oil prices, two costly wars in Yemen and Syria, and a demographic tidal wave (youth bulge), the Kingdom finds itself at a crossroads. Fundamental to its future success will be effective implementation of the 2030 Vision and an education system to support it that provides the necessary professional and cross-cultural skills to succeed in an increasingly integrated and competitive world.

———

Mr. POE. Thank you, Dr. Johnston. The Chair recognizes himself for some questions.

I want to be clear that when we are dealing with Saudi Arabia it is not all or nothing. Like I said earlier, they are the arsonists but they are also the firefighters when it comes to terrorism. That is what makes this very troubling, this whole issue.

And, Ms. Shea, let me start with you. If I understand correctly, Saudi Arabia agreed in 2006 that they would fix this problem and they would have it all fixed by 2008. Is that correct?

Ms. SHEA. Yes, Mr. Chairman. They——

Mr. POE. Okay. Reclaiming my time because I only have a few minutes.

So here it is now 9 years later and it is still not fixed, maybe some progress, but it is the issue that they promised in 2006 to fix the textbooks has not come about. Is that right?

Ms. SHEA. Yes, that is correct.

Mr. POE. So that is nine grades. That is almost a generation of students that they furnished the textbooks to that are still receiving this, in my opinion, violation of human rights.

Saudi Arabian schools teach religion and it is mandatory that all students go to these religious classes. Is that correct?

Ms. SHEA. Yes.

Mr. POE. And that is where these textbooks are used?

Ms. SHEA. Yes.

Mr. POE. And they are not only used in Saudi Arabia but they are used in other places in the world, including in the United States, as Congressman Wolf has stated; is that right?

Ms. SHEA. They have about 20 schools that they directly run. And then they are spread—for example, Dr. Johnston's report said that there were 150 schools that Saudi Arabia has established in Burkina Faso alone. So that gives you some, you know, some idea of the scale. It is all over the world, all continents and where there are people, where there are Muslim communities. And they are— not every one is receiving Saudi textbooks, but many, many are.

Mr. POE. And some say that the radicalization in Kosovo and Indonesia are a result of these textbooks being in these schools. Are you aware of that?

Ms. SHEA. Yes, I am. I hear it all the time.

Mr. POE. Congressman Wolf.

Mr. WOLF. Yes.

Mr. POE. Dr. Johnston, I know the State Department contracted with your group to study this issue, gave a grant, American taxpayer money, a grant for you all to study the issue. You studied it. You have got a report there in your hand. But the State Department still to this day refuses to release to the public that report. Is that correct?

Mr. JOHNSTON. No, that is not true, sir.

Mr. POE. So they have, they have released the report?

Mr. JOHNSTON. They have. But not, not on their own doing.

Mr. POE. It has been released because somebody leaked the report.

Mr. JOHNSTON. No. It was because the New York Times used the Freedom of Information Act to get a copy of the report.

Mr. POE. So it has been. The public does have access to your entire report?

Mr. JOHNSTON. Absolutely.

Mr. POE. All right. Thank you. I did not know that.

So, Congressman Wolf, let me ask you. You mentioned a few things that must be done. This has been going on for a good number of years. And where we are today, I think the United States—this is my opinion—doesn't want to endanger the sensitivities of our relationship with our Saudi allies. What would—how would you characterize this relationship and the demanding that we—that they change their textbooks?

Mr. WOLF. Well, it goes up and down. And during the area of oil crisis nobody wanted to offend the Saudis. America is fast becoming basically energy independent.

I think what you are doing with the hearing today by bringing the attention.

Two, there ought to be the new U.S. Ambassador for Religious Freedom, the person whose name I have heard is a very outstanding person who will be very good on this issue, the subcommittee should meet with that person.

Thirdly, you ought to have questions going over to the Senate Foreign Affairs Committee. When they send the name up of the new Ambassador there will be very tough questions from both sides of the aisle—this is not a political issue, if you will—aggressively putting him on record or her on record, whoever it is, that they will speak out.

Lastly, when he or she is confirmed this subcommittee ought, ought to meet with them.

And I think the more you pressure and do it publicly, in a very respectful way, you have to be careful, though, because the Saudis put a lot of money in different universities. They also hire prominent law firms in town. I couldn't believe, 3 weeks ago a prominent law firm was hired to represent Bashir, an indicted war criminal, indicted for genocide, responsible for the death of 200,000 to 300,000 people in Darfur, bombing people in the Nuba Mountains, and yet a law firm, prominent law firm working for him. So you have to be careful that there isn't pressure.

But what you have done today following up with it, I don't think the State Department will aggressively do it unless the Congress pushes them.

Mr. POE. Last question. Dr. Weinberg, you mentioned that 17 minutes into this hearing, that was a public notice that we were having this hearing, the Saudi Arabians did something. What did they do?

Mr. WEINBERG. They, they announced on social media that a new round of curriculum revisions had been completed which, again, needs to be not a justification for letting scrutiny off but a justification for added scrutiny to see if they have actually delivered on what they pledged.

If I could just add my voice to what the Honorable Mr. Wolf said about envoys. In addition to encouraging the administration to nominate a qualified individual for the congressionally-mandated post of Ambassador-at-Large for International Religious Freedom, there are four other important positions that are laying vacant on this issue right now.

There is currently no nominee, at least as of last I checked 2 days ago, for a U.S. Ambassador to Saudi Arabia. It should be somebody with real experience in the relationship and not just business experience.

Additionally, there is no nominee for the Special Representative of the State Department to Muslim Communities Abroad, a crucial vacancy.

Additionally, there is still no nominee, no nominee for the Anti-Semitism Envoy at the State Department. And the Secretary of State even suggested that such a nominee might be counter-productive for addressing anti-Semitism by taking it out of the priorities of the State Department, which I think is a deeply counter-productive perspective.

And then, lastly, there is the position of Ambassador for—or Special Envoy for Religious Freedom of Minorities in the Broader Middle East, a position that is mandated by Congress. There is somebody serving in this capacity but not with the level of seniority that Congress has mandated.

So those are all areas where you all can have an important voice.

Mr. POE. Four positions, four witnesses, I think maybe we can solve that problem right here.

I yield to the gentleman from Massachusetts, the ranking member Mr. Keating.

Mr. KEATING. Thank you, Mr. Chairman.

Dr. Johnston, you mentioned that the Center is moving forward and they are looking at three countries to see what the effect, do an in-depth examination of the religious and social impact of Saudi educational materials in those countries. Can you tell us and expand on what countries were chosen and what reason were those countries included in this study?

Mr. JOHNSTON. They have not been chosen. We are currently examining the feasibility of securing a memorandum of understanding with selected governments that would pass this test. These are going to be three countries of strategic consequence. They will be drawn from Southeast Asia, the Middle East, and Europe.

Mr. KEATING. Could you share any timetable that you might have?

Mr. JOHNSTON. I would say that we would, we would have this firmly underway within 2 months.

I would say, too, and I am sorry that time didn't permit this earlier, but in response to our study on the global impact, the Saudis actually put out a request to the Cultural Attaches of every one of their Embassies around the world encouraging them to, directing them to retrieve any old textbooks that might be in use within their respective geographic areas and to replace them with new.

The problem with that, of course, is the new still have problems. But this is to just show you that they are not deaf to the issue of this stuff going worldwide. And one of the things we are trying to do is just to impart a sense of ownership on all of that. And I think they are stepping up to the plate.

Mr. KEATING. Well, 9 years, they might be not be deaf but they are slow of hearing I would say in a sense.

Mr. JOHNSTON. It is glacial.

Mr. KEATING. Certainly.

And one of the concerns, too, when we are looking at this overall problem and the expansion of these materials, I think a lot rests on the control that the home country has on its education curriculum. I think Ms. Shea mentioned Burkina Faso and Mali.

And how much are countries like that reliant on these Saudi materials? Financially, what is the control? And this should seem to me an opportunity for the United States to try and deal with this directly. What opportunities could we have in those countries if they are reliant on money and resources for curriculum from Saudi Arabia, which we are learning today still contains material that is not, not appropriate, to say the least?

So, tell us about what your views are of the impact of those home-controlled countries on the curriculum?

Ms. SHEA. Yes, it is very determinant. I even spoke to an imam from a mosque in the United States about—who had Saudi textbooks in his library that he made available in the school. And he has since removed it he said. But he, he said that the reason why is that he didn't—he was working with an immigrant community that was impoverished, and that they do not have a school, they do not have textbooks, they do not have religious textbooks. So they turn to the country in the world with the deep pockets for such things. So they——

Mr. KEATING. Could I interrupt to say that given the U.S. interest here, isn't that a priority for our country perhaps? Is there an opportunity? Or would they not be receptive to the United States?

Ms. SHEA. Well, it is going to be very tricky. The United States cannot be funding religious things like that.

Mr. KEATING. How about through NGOs or funding through NGOs or anything like this?

Ms. SHEA. Well, I think the solution, again, is to force the—or press the Saudis to clean up their textbooks because they are going to be online. And——

Mr. KEATING. Well, if they are, if the Saudis are so sincere about this, what are they doing currently to the current generation and the prior generations that have been so indoctrinated in this material? Have they done anything in a remedial nature to deal with this whatsoever?

Mr. JOHNSTON. Well, one of the things they did in their deradicalization program is that they fired 3,000 imams. They retrained 20,000 others out of a total pool of 75,000 imams. So that is, that is taking care of it within their own borders.

Beyond that, the question that you asked where they have paid for the mosques and all the rest of it, you find in most countries they have significant control over what is taking place in the schools.

Again, I would just point out there is an important caveat here. That may not be the Government of Saudi Arabia very easily it seems. You know, peel back the onion, it is very difficult to follow.

Mr. KEATING. If I could——

Mr. JOHNSTON. But, but a more——

Mr. KEATING [continuing]. Just because my time is about to expire, if I could just—then you can have your chance with the committee to address that, a little bit of an expansion here.

Congressman Wolf mentioned some of the things directly he thought. He gave specifics about what the U.S. could do. Just in a very short summary, if any of you have specific, specific ideas I would like to hear them.

Mr. WEINBERG. So on the topic of exportation that we were just discussing, one thing that has always plagued this issue, and this was a challenge for that New York Times investigation that the chairman was discussing, I spoke with some of the reporters who were involved in that and related efforts at the Times, and one of the challenges when it comes to studying this exportation issue is there is often only anecdotal data or it is, you know, very, very vague and impressionistic.

So, one of the things that the U.S. Government can do to really play an important role here is to use all the assets of the U.S. Government on this, and in particular, the intelligence community. The easiest thing, or the most important thing that can be done in terms of informing this debate would simply be a directive from Congress to the intelligence community to monitor the exportation of incitement from Saudi Arabia, including but not limited to textbooks, and to direct them to report on this.

Additionally, Congress can call for rebooting the U.S.-Saudi strategic dialogue with a track to include issues related to incitement. And that rebooting, in a general sense, is something that the new crown prince of Saudi Arabia is reported to support.

And then, additionally, Congress can publicly and privately raise this issue, as well as urging the President to do so, and to issue a formal directive to U.S. agencies and cabinet members to do so as well.

Mr. KEATING. Thank you, Mr. Weinberg. In respect to my other committee members, if you can do that in writing——

Mr. JOHNSTON. Do you want any more ideas?

Mr. KEATING [continuing]. I think that would be helpful.

We might, but I have to be respectful of the other committee members, unless we have a second round. But anything like that I think the committee would appreciate in writing.

And, also, you know the committee is aware perhaps that there is classified material along the lines that Dr. Weinberg suggested that they may want to review, something that I think the committee might be interested in doing.

And I yield back, Mr. Chairman.

Mr. POE. I thank the gentleman.

The Chair recognizes the gentleman from Pennsylvania, Mr. Perry.

Mr. PERRY. Thanks, Mr. Chairman. Thanks to the panel here.

Mr. Weinberg, you mentioned a report in your testimony, or maybe in questions, I can't remember, but what is the report going to do? What is it going to do to Saudi Arabia and what is it—said report, so to speak, what would it do to the United States?

Mr. WEINBERG. So, one of the challenges of this issue to date is something that Ms. Shea addresses in her written testimony, which is the tendency of the State Department, because its priority is maintaining constructive relations with Saudi Arabia and advancing a range of other issues in the bilateral relationship such that they usually don't want to rock the boat, that a long-term strategic priority for the United States like textbooks doesn't get raised in the immediate term when it needs to get raised, and it gets kicked down the road indefinitely.

So as a result, State Department language on this issue every year in their International Religious Freedom Report, in their Human Rights Report, as well as in their country reports on terrorism such as the one that came out today, basically have a throw-away line or two about some incitement still remaining, without providing any specific examples typically, or at least without providing direct quotations. And so, and well——

Mr. PERRY. Is this not like widely known? Like, doesn't the whole world, like, we all know this; right? Everybody knows, everybody in the room knows this. With all due respect, I just, look, the report might be nice but I don't, I don't see it moving the ball quite honestly.

Mr. WEINBERG. Yes.

Mr. PERRY. I mean, maybe in the panoply of everything you are going to do that, you have to add that.

Mr. WEINBERG. If I could play devil's advocate for a moment. So, part of the challenge with this issue has been the absence of current data when people actually have their conversations with Saudi officials.

So, for example, the important study that Mr. Johnston's institute did, its results were not raised with Saudi officials by them or by the U.S. Government to the best of our knowledge——

Mr. PERRY. But that is the, that is——

Mr. WEINBERG [continuing]. Until the books were already obsolete.

Mr. PERRY. That is an issue of will, not of information. I mean, I have got textbook experts right in front—excerpts right in front of me here, so.

Mr. WEINBERG. But the reason those excerpts were done, until May most of those excerpts were not actually in the public sphere because nobody had gotten access to the books and sat down and read them and transcribed them.

Mr. PERRY. You are telling me that we legitimately——

Mr. WEINBERG. So for several years we didn't know.

Mr. PERRY. And I am not trying to be bellicose or difficult——

Mr. WEINBERG. Yeah.

Mr. PERRY [continuing]. But you are telling me we had no physical evidence like this——

Mr. WEINBERG. Right.

Mr. PERRY [continuing]. Until May 2017?

Mr. WEINBERG. For this academic year, yes.

Mr. PERRY. Oh, for this academic year. But we have for every other academic year back to 1970, 1980 or something.

Mr. WEINBERG. But just, just like that tweet from the Saudi Embassy that we were discussing, the Saudi Government every year claims that this has, this has been seriously worked over and so the stuff that people are concerned about is old news. And so it is important for the United States Government——

Mr. PERRY. Well, of course there is propaganda. I mean, you can listen to Russia T.V. and Al Jazeera as well if you want to believe all that stuff. But I mean, I hope that Americans are a little brighter than that.

Let me ask anybody this: Regarding incitement, because I just don't feel like we ever go far enough, and I am not sure even the suggestions I have heard go far enough to suit me—that is just me—but does anybody know whether incitement, you know, when you talk about the penalty for the adulterer who has previously consummated a marriage is stoning to death, that is in the book; or apostasy, you know, the penalty for apostasy is killing, that is, you know, that is in the textbook; you know, I don't know if this is incitement in the classic example or case. And I don't know if it meets the Brandenburg test.

Does anybody know if it does? Have we ever tried to? I mean, nobody wants to get into the suppression of free speech, but at some point free speech crosses over the line into incitement. Now, I guess the test is intended, likely, and imminent, and which the courts at some point decided what imminent was. Does anybody know whether that has ever been challenged? Have we ever taken a shot at it? Does the government have an interest?

Okay. Yes, ma'am.

Ms. SHEA. Well, I think, I think we have done that in the case of Americans who have posted such death threats against, like for example, the South Park cartoonist who did an irreverent cartoon of——

Mr. PERRY. But I am talking about the textbooks. Is this, is this,——

Ms. SHEA. But no, I mean I don't see how that——

Mr. PERRY [continuing]. Is this considered incitement?

Ms. SHEA. I don't see how that could be, I don't see how there is—there is diplomatic immunity—I don't see how the Saudi textbook.

Mr. PERRY. The textbook has diplomatic immunity?

Ms. SHEA. Well, they are published by the Government of Saudi Arabia who would be held responsible. The Ministry of Education of Saudi Arabia is the, the printer. And the Government of Saudi Arabia is the sponsor.

Mr. PERRY. So if the Government of Saudi Arabia publishes information that says that every, every citizen that has an affiliation with Saudi Arabia living in the United States should kill the next American they see, there is nothing we can do about that? Like we can't, we can't have that removed from the shelf because it is the Government of Saudi Arabia?

Ms. SHEA. Well, that is the—I mean, we have pressed people who actually carried out the crime. But it, you know——

Mr. PERRY. But incitement, there have been prosecutions for incitement in advance of the crime based on incitement; right? The question is has, to anybody's knowledge has anybody in the United States on behalf of the United States pursued that avenue regarding the textbooks and the passages therein as incitement?

Ms. SHEA. Some of the 9/11 victims' families may have been suing Saudi Arabia for reparations. But, but I don't know what the theory of their case was, whether it was the incitement.

Mr. PERRY. It seems like maybe either the answer is no or unknown. So maybe that is a place we can go into further.

Mr. Chairman, I yield back.

Mr. POE. I thank the gentleman from Pennsylvania.

The Chair will have one more round of 2 minutes per member. I will yield my time initially to the ranking member Mr. Keating from Massachusetts for his questions.

Mr. KEATING. Mr. Weinberg, you said one of the things that we can all do is speak up more and be consistent in doing it at every level. Taking into consideration what Congressman Wolf said, you know, there are generations of leaders before this, both sides of the aisle, that haven't been aggressive enough, as he testified.

However, President Trump was just in Saudi Arabia. President Trump was talking about extremism and the need to band together to do it. Yet there is no report that he brought this issue up in the course of that.

What is the danger in not bringing this up, particularly at that level, particularly under that thing?

Mr. WEINBERG. Yes. So this is, this is, this is the challenge is that the President almost never raises the issue. This was the case with President George W. Bush, this was the case with President Obama. This was the—appears to be the case with President Trump. Which is part of why the strategic dialogue was inaugurated between the U.S. and Saudi Arabia under the Bush administration so that senior officials could still raise priority concerns when it didn't rise to a level of the Commander-in-Chief as their number one, or two, or three priority but still needed to be addressed because of U.S. interests.

But that having been said, that is not an excuse for the President not to address it. It is not an excuse for the President not to direct cabinet members to do so as well.

President Trump, when he participated in the inauguration of a global center for combating extremist ideology in Saudi, while he was in Saudi Arabia—which by the way was in the works for 2 years and then they repackaged it to be a deliverable during this summit—he predicted it would make history.

Reflecting on his visit to the Kingdom several weeks later, he urged all nations to stop teaching people to kill other people, stop filling their minds with hate and intolerance. And he said he would not name other countries besides Qatar.

Now, I actually have an article draft forthcoming which explains why Qatar's record on counterterrorism issues is actually worse than all of its other neighbors in the Gulf monarchies. But that having been said, the books need to be addressed directly, with knowledge, on a regular basis with current information about the current school year, or else it is not going to have any impact with the Saudi Government. Otherwise, the Saudi Government is going to keep doing what it is doing, which is reprinting these books year after year with incitement, and indoctrinating, you know, at least several more years of students with this problematic information.

Mr. JOHNSTON. May I correct the record on something? This report was in fact—I briefed the Saudis in Riyadh on this report. It was sent over through diplomatic channels as well. And out of that came one ray of hope.

We worked for several years on one of the recommendations which was to bring Saudi educators together with American educators to deal with the problem of bias and intolerance in national education systems. Out of this came a series of recommendations to their government, and our own, but to their government which I delivered to their Minister of Education.

One of the things I feel is so important, and it hasn't been mentioned here, but far more important than these textbooks, far more important is the teacher training. And we have opportunities now to be able to go over there and in the context of this national plan for educational reform, which was crafted mostly by McKinsey & Company, it is a dynamite plan, and if they fully implement it it will actually leapfrog some of our own habits. But I think there the door is open that we could go and help them implement this and particularly get at the teacher training, which is, as I say, far more important.

Mr. KEATING. I yield back.

Mr. POE. I thank the gentleman.

The Chair recognizes the gentleman from Pennsylvania, Mr. Perry.

Mr. PERRY. Thanks, Mr. Chairman.

Mr. Johnston, Dr. Johnston, I understand one of the problems for the United States is how the actions, the statements versus actions coming from Saudi Arabia are determined. And I indeed asked the Secretary about the metrics to determine efficacy of the Saudi's actions and how we are measuring their progress.

I will tell you now—well, the man's been on the job for 4 or 5 months, right, so we have to give him some leeway—but I didn't get a lot of confidence that anything meaningful was there. And I actually wonder, some of the officials who may be determining whether what the efficacy is, literally that might be, I hate to say it, but so to speak working for the other side.

So, in your work with the, the ICRD how would you characterize the metrics we use and who is determining? Is it, it is appropriate or is that problematic that—that needs to be addressed? And where is that addressed?

Mr. JOHNSTON. No, I, I think one of the metrics is the baseline that we established here back in 2011. To be sure, we haven't looked at those books in 5 years. But the U.S. Commission on International Religious Freedom did several years ago. We provided them the baseline.

They determined that further reform was taking place. And in this year's annual report they even talk about a visit there in February of this year where they determined that more reform was taking place. So this is a metric.

We are going to be looking very hard at it starting in another month on the high school grades. That is where most of the onerous content exists.

And one of the other things in terms about why this is so slow is they took a full year to field test their revisions to the 10th grade, which was, as far as we were concerned, was the one grade where it was the worst. And they did those revisions. I don't know what has come of that. We will find out. But they did take a full year to test it.

And the other thing we have to remember is that a lot of this is getting in on religious grounds. And some of that is pretty——

Mr. PERRY. But I think they use that. And good for them, I suppose.

Mr. JOHNSTON. Sometimes yes. Yes.

Mr. PERRY. But it is an Achilles heel for the United States. And we can't allow that to be used against us, especially for what many consider to be seditious activity.

And I also would question what progress means or what, you know, reforms are taking place at what level. I mean, reform, you know, they might change one word in that sentence and of course they reformed the sentence, I guess in this classic, very strict constructionist sense. But from the greater sense and the spirit of it, it is not getting the job done and it is not getting done quickly enough for us.

And what they do in their country, quite honestly and quite frankly from my opinion, that is their business, but what they do in our country is our business.

Mr. JOHNSTON. Yes. No, your points are very valid.

One thing I would say is in addition to eliminating negative content, one of the things we have found, and we just took a quick glance, there is the addition of very positive content that sort of works in the other direction.

I don't know to what extent they are constrained by this needing to keep their religious establishment on board, because that is where they get their, their authority from is from the religious establishment. That is part of the package. So it is a difficult walk that they are making. The people that I have worked with I am 1,000 percent convinced are very sincere. And, in fact, one of them——

Mr. PERRY. With the chairman's indulgence, I agree, in their country it is inexorably linked since they came to power, the House of Saud. And I get all that and why the need to keep, to do all the things they need to do. I don't agree with it but I understand it.

However, in this country none of it is appropriate, none of it is appropriate and we should take action.

Thank you, Mr. Chairman.

Mr. POE. I thank the gentleman.

Congressman Wolf, I have a question for you first and then I will let you make a comment because I know you want to keep, you want to talk about the last question.

ISIS used Saudi Arabian textbooks up until 2015. That was 2 years ago. And now they use their own textbooks. Would you like to comment on where ISIS gets—got their textbooks to begin with?

Mr. WOLF. Well, you are right. In the New York Times piece they say, "In a huge embarrassment to the Saudi authorities, the Islamic State adopted official Saudi textbooks for its schools until the extremist group could publish its own textbooks in 2015."

Secondly, when I was in 2 years ago we went up into the Nineveh Plains. We went into meetings with all the different people. At every meeting I said, Tell me, who is helping the Saudis—rather, who is helping ISIS? And every meeting, every meeting two came up, some three, but two came up: The Saudis, not always the Saudi Government but Saudi individuals, and he sort of alluded to the renegade guy; secondly, Qatar. They were aiding and abetting ISIS. And there was another country, Turkey, who was for the longest period of time was allowing people, they go to Istanbul, they call a telephone number, they go south and they join.

They may have changed. But don't forget, 15 of the 19 hijackers were from Saudi Arabia. Bin Laden was from Saudi Arabia. The number of people from my area who were killed in the attack on the Pentagon, the guys who did it, Saudi Arabia.

And so I think what this committee has done today with the hearing, the textbooks are important, but all these issues, and you push and you push and you push. And I urge you to meet with the new ambassador, and I urge you to sit down with him or her, who-ever it is, and pressure them, and the new religious freedom am-bassador. I think you may have started something here.

And the real danger is you even recall last year—I read the 28 pages—you remember last year the issue came up, the Saudis hired law firms and PR firms in this town to do everything. Fortu-nately the Congress, to its good credit, passed it and was not influ-enced. But you know what is going on, so by this hearing you can cover all the textbooks are important but terrorism is important. All these things are very, very important. And, hopefully, this can be the genesis if you guys, men and women, continue to really make a difference and stop what Saudi Arabia has been doing for a long period of time.

Mr. POE. Thank you. And the ranking member and I will request a meeting with the Ambassador and we will go from there. Maybe have a hearing in the future on Qatar, have all of you back.

And I want to have one last question for all four of you. Since we are talking about textbooks and schools, how would you rank the—at this time—the goal of changing the textbooks so that they don't preach hate, intolerance, and violence? And it is real simple, it is not pass or fail, it is A, B, C, D, or F.

You understand the question, Ms. Shea? How would you rank what Saudi Arabia is doing right now?

Ms. SHEA. F.

Mr. POE. All right. Dr. Weinberg?

Mr. WEINBERG. F with credit for effort.

Mr. POE. F with credit for effort. Okay.

Congressman Wolf?

Mr. WOLF. F plus instead of F.

Mr. POE. Dr. Johnston?

Mr. JOHNSTON. I would give it a D.

And one of the things I would point out is that as long as we are, you know, buying 150 billion—selling $150 billion worth of arms to the Saudis, they are not going to pay a whole lot of attention to western criticism. When you couple that reality with the line they are walking with the religious establishment, I think that they are making as much progress as one could hope for at this point in time.

They need to do a lot better, but there is, there is sincere desire to do better on their part, the government's part. I don't know about the religious.

Mr. POE. And without belaboring the point, if we take Ms. Shea's recommendation, we tie defense contracts to Saudi Arabia with the repairing of their textbooks, that may get somebody's attention. I don't know. We will see.

Anyway, I want to thank all of you for being here. I want to thank all of the people in the audience for being here as well.

And this subcommittee is adjourned.

[Whereupon, at 3:56 p.m., the subcommittee was adjourned.]

APPENDIX

Material Submitted for the Record

SUBCOMMITTEE HEARING NOTICE
COMMITTEE ON FOREIGN AFFAIRS
U.S. HOUSE OF REPRESENTATIVES
WASHINGTON, DC 20515-6128

Subcommittee on Terrorism, Nonproliferation, and Trade
Ted Poe (R-TX), Chairman

TO: MEMBERS OF THE COMMITTEE ON FOREIGN AFFAIRS

You are respectfully requested to attend an OPEN hearing of the Committee on Foreign Affairs, to be held jointly by the Subcommittee on Terrorism, Nonproliferation, and Trade in Room 2200 of the Rayburn House Office Building (and available live on the Committee website at http://www.ForeignAffairs.house.gov):

DATE: Wednesday, July 19, 2017

TIME: 2:15 p.m.

SUBJECT: Saudi Arabia's Troubling Educational Curriculum

WITNESSES: Ms. Nina Shea
                   Director
                   Center for Religious Freedom
                   Hudson Institute

                   David A. Weinberg, Ph.D.
                   Senior Fellow
                   Foundation for Defense of Democracies

                   The Honorable Frank Wolf
                   Distinguished Senior Fellow
                   21st Century Wilberforce Initiative
                   (Former U.S. Representative)

                   Douglas Johnston, Ph.D.
                   President Emeritus
                   International Center for Religion and Diplomacy

By Direction of the Chairman

The Committee on Foreign Affairs seeks to make its facilities accessible to persons with disabilities. If you are in need of special accommodations, please call 202/225-5021 at least four business days in advance of the event, whenever practicable. Questions with regard to special accommodations in general (including availability of Committee materials in alternative formats and assistive listening devices) may be directed to the Committee.

COMMITTEE ON FOREIGN AFFAIRS

MINUTES OF SUBCOMMITTEE ON _______ *Terrorism, Nonproliferation, and Trade* _______ HEARING

Day __*Wednesday*__ Date _____ *7/19/17* _____ Room _____ *2200* _____

Starting Time _____ *2:45* _____ Ending Time _____ *3:56* _____

Recesses ____ (___ to ___) (___ to ___) (___ to ___) (___ to ___) (___ to ___) (___ to ___)

Presiding Member(s)

Chairman Ted Poe

Check all of the following that apply:

Open Session [✓]
Executive (closed) Session [ ]
Televised [ ]

Electronically Recorded (taped) [✓]
Stenographic Record [✓]

TITLE OF HEARING:

"Saudi Arabia's Troubling Educational Curriculum"

SUBCOMMITTEE MEMBERS PRESENT:

Reps. Poe, Keating, Wilson, Titus, Cook, Torres, Perry, Schneider, Zeldin, Mast, Garrett

NON-SUBCOMMITTEE MEMBERS PRESENT: *(Mark with an * if they are not members of full committee.)*

HEARING WITNESSES: Same as meeting notice attached? Yes [✓] No [ ]
(If "no", please list below and include title, agency, department, or organization.)

STATEMENTS FOR THE RECORD: *(List any statements submitted for the record.)*

IFR submitted by Mr. Wolf
IFR submitted by Mr. Weinberg

TIME SCHEDULED TO RECONVENE _______
or
TIME ADJOURNED _____ *3:56* _____

____
Subcommittee Staff Associate

MATERIAL SUBMITTED FOR THE RECORD BY DAVID A. WEINBERG, PH.D., SENIOR FELLOW, FOUNDATION FOR DEFENSE OF DEMOCRACIES

قـررت وزارة الـتعـليـم تـدريس
هـذا الكـتاب وطـبعـه على نفقنها

وزارة التعليم
Ministry of Education

المملكة العربية السعودية
وزارة التعليم

التعليـم الثـانـوي
(نظـام الـمقـررات)
البرنامج المشترك

قـام بالتأليف والمراجعة
فريق من المتخصصين

يوزع مجاناً ولا يباع

طبعة ١٤٣٧ ــ ١٤٣٨ هـ

ح وزارة التعليم ، ١٤٢٧ هـ

فهرسة مكتبة الملك فهد الوطنية أثناء النشر
وزارة التعليم
فقه ١ (التعليم الثانوي) - الرياض ١٤٢٧ هـ
٢٩٢ ص ؛ ٢١ × ٢٥,٥ سم
ردمك : ٦ ـ ٢٤٥ ـ ٤٨ ـ ٩٩٦٠
١ ـ العبادات (فقه اسلامي) ـ كتب دراسية   ٢ ـ الفقه الإسلامي ـ كتب دراسية
٣ ـ التعليم الثانوي ـ السعودية ـ كتب دراسية   أ ـ العنوان
ديوي ٧١٢، ٢٥٢   ١٤٢٧ / ٣٧٩٥

رقم الايداع : ٣٧٩٥ / ١٤٢٧
ردمك : ٦ ـ ٢٤٥ ـ ٤٨ ـ ٩٩٦٠

لهذا المقرر قيمة مهمة وفائدة كبيرة فلنحافظ عليه، ولنجعل نظافته تشهد على حسن سلوكنا معه

اذا لم نحتفظ بهذا المقرر في مكتبتنا الخاصة في آخر العام للاستفادة، فلنجعل مكتبة مدرستنا تحتفظ به.

حقوق الطبع والنشر محفوظة لوزارة التعليم، المملكة العربية السعودية

موقع
www.moe.gov.sa

البريد الإلكتروني
لقسم العلوم الشرعية ـ الإدارة العامة للمناهج
islamic.cur@moe.gov.sa

حد الزاني المحصن (الثيب)

حد الزاني المحصن هو الرجم بالحجارة حتى يموت بإجماع أهل السنة.

وقد دل على ذلك السنة المتواترة القطعية من قول النبي ﷺ وفعله، وإجماع الأمة.

فمن ذلك ما روى عبادة بن الصامت ﷺ قال: قال رسول الله ﷺ : «خذوا عني خذوا عني، قد جعل الله لهن سبيلاً، البكر بالبكر جلد مائة ونفي سنة، والثيب بالثيب جلد مائة والرجم، [1]. وعن عمر بن الخطاب ﷺ أنه قال : إن الله تعالى بعث محمداً ﷺ بالحق وأنزل عليه الكتاب فكان فيما أنزل عليه آية الرجم، فقرأناها وعقلناها ووعيناها، ورجم رسول الله ﷺ ورجمنا بعده [2].

وثبت أنه ﷺ رجم ماعزاً الأسلمي، وغيره.

والمحصن هو : من وطئ امرأته في نكاح صحيح، وهما بالغان عاقلان حران، فإن اختل شرط منها في أحد الزوجين فلا إحصان لواحد منهما.

حد الزنى غير المحصن (البكر)

إذا زنى الحر غير المحصن جلد مائة وغرب عاماً؛ لقوله سبحانه :

﴿ ٱلزَّانِيَةُ وَٱلزَّانِي فَٱجْلِدُوا۟ كُلَّ وَٰحِدٍ مِّنْهُمَا مِا۟ئَةَ جَلْدَةٍ ﴾ [3]، ولحديث عبادة المتقدم.

وغير المحصن هو من تخلف فيه أحد شروط الإحصان المتقدمة.

وإنما شددت العقوبة على المحصن وخففت على غير المحصن لأمور:

الأول : أن دواعي الزنا في حق المحصن أضعف، فهو قد تيسر له الزواج الذي يحصل به العفاف.

والثاني : أن في زنا المحصن خيانة للعلاقة الزوجية، وهدماً للأسرة.

والثالث : أن الأضرار الناشئة عن زنا المحصن أكثر، كانتقال الأمراض بين الزوجين، واختلاط الأنساب.

---

(١) أخرجه مسلم في كتاب الحدود باب حد الزنا برقم (٣١٩٩). وقوله : (البكر بالبكر) و(الثيب بالثيب). خرج مخرج الغالب أن البكر يزني بالبكر، والثيب يزني بالثيب، فلو زنى الثيب بالبكر فيرجم الثيب ويجلد البكر .

(٢) أخرجه البخاري في كتاب الحدود باب رجم الحبلى من الزنا إذا أحصنت برقم (٦٢٢٨) . ومسلم في كتاب الحدود باب رجم الثيب في الزنا برقم (٣٢٠١).

(٣) سورة النور، الآيتان ٣٠و٢١ .

الحكمة من تحريم الزنا

لا يخفى على عاقل ما في الزنا من الآثار السيئة، والمفاسد الوخيمة، على الأفراد والمجتمعات. والمتأمل في حال المجتمعات الغربية التي انتشرت فيها هذه الفاحشة يدرك عظمة التشريع الرباني الذي حذر المسلمين من مقاربته فضلاً عن الوقوع فيه.

فمن مفاسد هذه الجريمة :

١. اختلاط الأنساب الذي يبطل معه التعارف والتناصر على إحياء الدين، وتفكك الأسر، وضياع الأولاد.

٢. انتشار الأمراض في المجتمع [1]، ولهذا جاء في الحديث : «وما ظهرت الفاحشة في قوم قط إلا ابتلاهم الله بالأمراض والأوجاع التي لم تكن في أسلافهم» [2].

٣. القضاء على النكاح الذي هو من أهم مقاصد الشريعة.

٤. إدخال العار على الأسرة بل والقبيلة برمتها.

بالتعاون مع مجموعتك:

١/ توصل إلى مفاسد أخرى من المفاسد الكثيرة المترتبة على جريمة الزنا.

____

____

____

٢/ ما أسباب الوقوع في جريمة الزنا؟ وما سبل الوقاية من ذلك؟

سبل الوقاية من ذلك	أسباب الوقوع في جريمة الزنا

____

(١) كالأمراض التي ظهرت حديثاً مثل الإيدز والزهري وغيرها.

(٢) رواه ابن ماجه ١٣٣٢/٢ (٤٠١٩)، والحاكم في مستدركه ٥٨٣/٤ وقال : هذا حديث صحيح الإسناد ولم يخرجاه.

حَدُّ اللواط

ذهب جمهور الفقهاء أن حَدَّ اللواط، كحد الزنى.

من خلال دراستك لموضوع حَدِّ الزنى، وضّح حَدَّ اللواط بالتفصيل.

حَدُّ اللواط للمحصن :

....

حَدُّ اللواط لغير المحصن :

....

وقال بعض العلماء : عقوبة اللواط : القتل، فيقتل الفاعل والمفعول به، سواء أكانا محصنين أم غير محصنين .

قال شيخ الإسلام ابن تيمية رحمه الله؛ (والصحيح الذي اتفقت عليه الصحابة: أن يقتل الاثنان الأعلى والأسفل، سواء كانا محصنين، أم غير محصنين. فإن أهل السنن رووا عن ابن عباس رضي الله تعالى عنهما، عن النبي ﷺ قال: ((من وجدتموه يعمل عمل قوم لوط، فاقتلوا الفاعل والمفعول به)) (١)،(٢) .

الحكمة من تغليظ عقوبته

حرم الله اللواط وغلظ في عقوبته لما له من آثار سيئة على الفرد والمجتمع :

فهو انتكاسة في الفطرة، وفساد في الطبع، يقتل الفضيلة، ويهدم الأخلاق. يورث في نفس مرتكبه الرذيلة والدناءة، فيقضي على الحياء، ويميت الغيرة في النفوس.

من ارتكب هذه الجريمة لم يزل يعير بها بين الناس في حياته، ولم يفارق خزيها مخيلته حتى وفاته. ولا يقف عارها على مرتكبها فقط، بل يمتد ليشمل الأسرة والقبيلة برمتها.

وإذا ظهر اللواط في مجتمع فإن الله يعاجل أهله بالعقوبة، فتحل الكوارث والأسقام، وتنتشر الأوبئة والأمراض، ويخيم الظلم ويعم الفساد في الأرض، نسأل الله السلامة والعافية.

نشاط

ما أسباب الوقوع في جريمة اللواط؟ وما سبل الوقاية من ذلك؟

أسباب الوقوع في جريمة اللواط	سبل الوقاية من ذلك

---

(١) أخرجه أحمد ٤٦٤/٤ (٢٧٣٢)، و أبو داوود في كتاب الحدود، بابٌ فيمَنْ عَمِلَ عَمَلَ قوم لوط ١٥٨/٤ (٤٤٦٢)، والترمذي في أبواب الحدود، باب ما جاء في حَدّ اللوطي ٥٧/٤ (١٤٥٦)، وابن ماجه في كتاب الحدود، باب من عَمِلَ عَمَلَ قوم لوط ٨٥٦/٧ (٢٥٦١)، وصححه الحاكم في المستدرك على الصحيحين ٤٩٥/٤ والضياء في الأحاديث المختارة ٢٠٤/١٢، وابن عبد الهادي (المحرر في الحديث ص٦٢٤)، والألباني في إرواء الغليل (٢٢٥٠)، وقال ابن القيم: احتجّ الإمام أحمد بهذا الحديث، وإسنادُه على شرط البخاري. اهـ

(٢) السياسة الشرعية ص١٣٨.

أنواع الردة :

يحصل الكفر بأحد أمور :

١ / الردة بالقول، مثل : الاستهزاء بالله أو برسوله أو بدينه، ودعاء غير الله.

٢ / الردة بالفعل، مثل التقرب لغير الله بسجود أو ذبح ونحو ذلك، والسحر فإنه كفر؛ لقوله تعالى : ﴿ وَمَا كَفَرَ سُلَيْمَٰنُ وَلَٰكِنَّ ٱلشَّيَٰطِينَ كَفَرُواْ يُعَلِّمُونَ ٱلنَّاسَ ٱلسِّحْرَ ﴾ [1]، والكهانة، وهي ادعاء علم الغيب، إذ لا يعلم الغيب إلا الله.

٣ / الردة بالاعتقاد، مثل : اعتقاد الشريك له تعالى، وبغض النبي ﷺ أو بغض شريعته، واتخاذ وسائط بينه وبين الله يتوكل عليهم ويدعوهم ويستغيث بهم، وإنكار أمر معلوم من الدين بالضرورة، مثل إنكار البعث أو الجنة أو النار، واستباحة الزنا أو الخمر ونحو ذلك.

أنواع الردة

يحصل الكفر بأحد أمور :

١	الردة بالقول
٢	الردة بالفعل
٣	الردة بالاعتقاد

نشاط

بيّن ما هو ردة وما ليس كذلك في الأمثلة التالية، مع ذكر السبب :

التعليل	الحكم	المثال
		شخص يبيح الزنا
		شخص يدعي النبوة
		شخص ينكر عذاب القبر
		شخص يتعامل بالربا
		شخص زانٍ
		شخص يبيح الخمر
		شخص يصدق الكهان في معرفة الغيب

---

(١) سورة البقرة الآية ١٠٢.

عقوبة المرتد في الدنيا

حد الردة هو القتل، لا فرق في ذلك بين الرجل والمرأة، وقد ورد في السنة عدة نصوص تؤكد هذا الحكم.

بمراجعة بعض مصادر التعلم اذكر واحدا منها.

ولا يجوز قتله حتى يستتاب ثلاثة أيام على الأقل لعله يراجع دينه، وبهذا يفتح له باب التوبة، فإن تاب لم يجز قتله. وإن أصر على كفره قتل.

فإن تاب كفر الله عنه خطيئته، ولم يحبط عمله السابق؛ لقوله تعالى: ﴿ وَٱلَّذِينَ لَا يَدْعُونَ مَعَ ٱللَّهِ إِلَٰهًا ءَاخَرَ وَلَا يَقْتُلُونَ ٱلنَّفْسَ ٱلَّتِي حَرَّمَ ٱللَّهُ إِلَّا بِٱلْحَقِّ وَلَا يَزْنُونَ وَمَن يَفْعَلْ ذَٰلِكَ يَلْقَ أَثَامًا ۝ يُضَٰعَفْ لَهُ ٱلْعَذَابُ يَوْمَ ٱلْقِيَٰمَةِ وَيَخْلُدْ فِيهِۦ مُهَانًا ۝ إِلَّا مَن تَابَ وَءَامَنَ وَعَمِلَ عَمَلًا صَٰلِحًا فَأُوْلَٰئِكَ يُبَدِّلُ ٱللَّهُ سَيِّئَاتِهِمْ حَسَنَٰتٍ وَكَانَ ٱللَّهُ غَفُورًا رَّحِيمًا ۝ ﴾ [1].

عقوبته في الآخرة

إذا مات المرتد على ردته فعقوبته هي الخلود في النار وحبوط عمله الصالح الذي عمله قبل ردته؛ لقوله تعالى: ﴿ وَمَن يَرْتَدِدْ مِنكُمْ عَن دِينِهِۦ فَيَمُتْ وَهُوَ كَافِرٌ فَأُوْلَٰئِكَ حَبِطَتْ أَعْمَٰلُهُمْ فِي ٱلدُّنْيَا وَٱلْءَاخِرَةِ وَأُوْلَٰئِكَ أَصْحَٰبُ ٱلنَّارِ هُمْ فِيهَا خَٰلِدُونَ ۝ ﴾ [2].

أحكام المرتد

المرتد كافر، فيعامل معاملة الكفار، ومن ذلك أنه يفرق بينه وبين زوجته، ولا تؤكل ذبيحته، ولا يرث ولا يورث، ولا يغسل ولا يكفن ولا يصلى عليه ولا يدفن في مقابر المسلمين.

---

(١) سورة الفرقان الآيات ٦٨-٧٠.
(٢) سورة البقرة الآية ٢١٧.

قـــررت وزارة الـتـعـلـيـم تـدريـس
هـذا الكـتـاب وطـبـعـه عـلـى نـفـقـتـهـا

المملكة العربية السعودية
وزارة التعليم

التعليم الثانوي
(نظام المقررات)
البرنامج المشترك

قام بالتأليف والمراجعة

فريق من المتخصصين

يُوزع مجاناً ولا يُباع

طبعة ١٤٣٧ ــ ١٤٣٨هـ

Note: All pages of this material are not reprinted here but may be found in its entirety at http://docs.house.gov/Committee/Calendar/ByEvent.aspx?EventID=106289

MATERIAL SUBMITTED FOR THE RECORD BY THE HONORABLE FRANK WOLF, DISTIN-
GUISHED SENIOR FELLOW, 21ST CENTURY WILBERFORCE INITIATIVE (FORMER U.S.
REPRESENTATIVE)

7/17/2017   Saudi Arabia: USCIRF Confirms Material Inciting Violence, Intolerance Remains in Textbooks Used at Saudi Government's Islamic Saudi Acade…

United States Commission *on*
International Religious Freedom

Saudi Arabia: USCIRF Confirms Material Inciting Violence, Intolerance Remains in Textbooks Used at Saudi Government's Islamic Saudi Academy

FOR IMMEDIATE RELEASE

June 11, 2008

Contact: Judith Ingram
Communications Director
(202) 523-3240, ext. 127
communications@uscirf.gov

WASHINGTON—Last fall, the United States Commission on International Religious Freedom asked the U.S. Department of State to secure the release of all Arabic-language textbooks used at a Saudi government school in Northern Virginia, the Islamic Saudi Academy (ISA). The Commission took this action in order to ensure that the books be publicly examined to determine whether the texts used at the ISA promote violence, discrimination, or intolerance based on religion or belief. The ISA is unlike any conventional private or parochial school in the United States in that it is operated by a foreign government and uses that government"s official texts. It falls under the Commission"s mandate to monitor the actions of foreign governments in relation to religious freedom. The government of Saudi Arabia, as a member of the international community, is committed to upholding international standards, including the obligation not to promote violence, intolerance, or hate.

The Commission requested Saudi government textbooks repeatedly during and following its trip to Saudi Arabia in May–June 2007. Shortly after the Commission raised the issue publicly, the Saudi government turned over textbooks used at the ISA to the State Department, but as of this writing, the Department has not made them available either to the public or to the Commission, nor has it released any statement about the content of the books that it received. Nevertheless, although it was unable to obtain the entire collection, the Commission managed to acquire and review 17 ISA textbooks in use during this school year from other, independent sources, including a congressional office. While the texts represent just a small fraction of the books used in this Saudi government school, the Commission"s review confirmed that these texts do, in fact, include some extremely troubling passages that do not conform to international human rights norms. The Commission calls once again for the full public release of all the Arabic-language textbooks used at the ISA.

In July 2006, the Saudi government confirmed to the U.S. government that, among other policies to improve religious freedom and tolerance, it would, within one to two years, "revise and update textbooks to remove remaining references that disparage Muslims or non-Muslims or that promote hatred toward other religions or religious groups." The Commission is releasing this statement as the two-year timeframe is coming to an end, and with particular concern over the content of textbooks used at the ISA, in order to highlight reforms that should be made before the 2008–09 school year begins at the ISA.

Examples of Problematic Passages in Current ISA Textbooks

The most problematic texts involve passages that are not directly from the Koran but rather contain the Saudi government"s particular interpretation of Koranic and other Islamic texts. Some passages clearly exhort the readers to commit acts of violence, as can be seen in the following two examples:

- In a twelfth-grade *Tafsir* (Koranic interpretation) textbook, the authors state that it is permissible for a Muslim to kill an apostate (a convert from Islam), an adulterer, or someone who has murdered a believer intentionally: "He (praised is He) prohibits killing the soul that God has forbidden (to kill) unless for just cause..." Just cause is then defined in the text as "unbelief after belief, adultery, and killing an inviolable believer intentionally." (*Tafsir*, Arabic/Sharia, 123)

- A twelfth-grade *Tawhid* (monotheism) textbook states that "[m]ajor polytheism makes blood and wealth permissible," which in Islamic legal terms means that a Muslim can take the life and property of someone believed to be guilty of this alleged transgression with impunity. (*Tawhid*, Arabic/Sharia, 15) Under the Saudi interpretation of Islam, "major polytheists" include Shi"a and Sufi Muslims, who visit the shrines of their saints to ask for intercession with God on their behalf, as well as Christians, Jews, Hindus, and Buddhists.

The overt exhortations to violence found in these passages make other statements that promote intolerance troubling even though they do not explicitly call for violent action. These other statements vilify adherents of the Ahmadi, Baha"i, and Jewish religions, as well as of Shi"a Islam. This is despite the fact that the Saudi government is obligated as a member of the United Nations and a state party to the International Convention on the Elimination of All Forms of Racial Discrimination and other relevant treaties to guarantee the right to freedom of thought, conscience, and religion. The statements include the following:

- "Today, Qadyanis [Ahmadis] are one of the greatest strongholds for spreading aberration, deviation, and heresy in the name of religion, even from within Islamic countries. Thus, the Qadyani [Ahmadi] movement has become a force of destruction and internal corruption today in the Islamic world..." ("Aspects of Muslim Political and Cultural History," Eleventh Grade, Administrative/Social Track, Sharia/Arabic Track, 99)

- "It [Baha"ism] is one of the destructive esoteric sects in the modern age... It has become clear that Babism [the precursor to Baha"ism], Baha"ism, and Qadyanism [Ahmadism] represent wayward forces inside the Islamic world that seek to strike it from within and weaken it.

They are colonial pillars in our Islamic countries and among the true obstacles to a renaissance." ("Aspects of Muslim Political and Cultural History," Eleventh Grade, 99–100)

- "The cause of the discord: The Jews conspired against Islam and its people. A sly, wicked person who sinfully and deceitfully professed Islam infiltrated (the Muslims). He was 'Abd Allah b. Saba" (from the Jews of Yemen). [_____]* began spewing his malice and venom against the third of the Rightly-Guided Caliphs, 'Uthman (may God be pleased with him), and falsely accused him." (*Tawhid*, Administrative/Social Sciences Track, 67)
  (*The word or words here were obscured by correction fluid.)

- Sunni Muslims are told to "shun those who are extreme regarding the People of the House (Muhammad"s family) and who claim infallibility for them." (*Tawhid*, Arabic/Sharia 82; *Tawhid*, Administrative/Social Sciences Track, 65) This would include all Shi"a Muslims, for whom the doctrine of infallibility is a cardinal principle.

Other problematic passages employ ambiguous language, and the textbook authors do nothing to clarify the meaning.

- A ninth-grade *Hadith* textbook states: "It is not permissible to violate the blood, property, or honor of the unbeliever who makes a compact with the Muslims. The blood of the mu"ahid is not permissible unless for a legitimate reason…the mu"ahid is an unbeliever who contracts a treaty with a Muslim providing for the safety of his life, property, and family." (*Hadith*, Ninth Grade, 142–3)

The passages about the *mu"ahid* are most troubling for what they leave out. They address the protected status of an unbeliever in a Muslim country, but are silent on whether unbelievers living in non-Muslim countries are afforded the same protections of "blood, property, or honor." Such an omission, taken together with the outright incitement to violence and vilifying language noted above, could be interpreted as tacitly condoning violence against non-Muslims living in non-Muslim countries.

The Commission would urge the textbook authors to put more context into some sections of the textbooks to avoid any perception that they could be encouraging violence. For example, one passage that requires clarification is the following explication of the Koranic phrase, "Respond to God and His Messenger when He calls you to that which will give you life." (Q 8:24)

Although this Koranic passage does not in itself invoke the term *jihad*, the Saudi textbook authors write:

- "In these verses is a call for jihad, which is the pinnacle of Islam. In (*jihad*) is life for the body; thus it is one of the most important causes of outward life. Only through force and victory over the enemies is there security and repose. Within martyrdom in the path of God (exalted and glorified is He) is a type of noble life-force that is not diminished by fear or poverty." (*Tafsir*, Arabic/Sharia, 68)

While there are various meanings of the term *jihad*, including an internal struggle of the soul, none are given in this brief discussion, which also includes an emphasis on the importance of power or force over one"s enemies and discusses "martyrdom" with approval. Such an ambiguous interpretation can be perceived as giving the verse a militant connotation, potentially justifying acts of violence, which should not be left without elucidation in a textbook that is aimed at children who are still learning the main tenets of religion.

More broadly, the analysis of the ills of the Muslim world that is offered in the ISA textbooks–that it was strong when united under a single caliph, a single language (Arabic), and a single creed (Sunnism), and that it has grown weak because of foreign influence and internal religious and ethnic divisions–is identical to some of the exclusionary ideological arguments used by extremists to justify acts of terror.

In the Commission"s view, these troubling passages should be modified, clarified, or removed altogether from the next edition of the textbooks in order to bring the books at this Saudi government school into conformity with international human rights standards.

Long-term Commission Concern over Content of Saudi Government Textbooks

The Commission has long called for Saudi Arabia to be designated a "country of particular concern," or CPC, for its egregious and systematic violations of religious freedom. In particular, the Commission has expressed concern about the promotion of religious intolerance and religion-based violence in official Saudi government textbooks used both within Saudi Arabia and at Saudi schools abroad, such as the ISA. The Commission has been urging the U.S. government to press the Saudi government to promote religious tolerance in the Saudi curriculum since 2001, and in 2003 it issued an in-depth report about religious freedom conditions in Saudi Arabia, including intolerance and incitement to violence found in Saudi textbooks and the country"s official educational curriculum. It was not until September 2004 that the State Department first publicly expressed concern over the Saudi government"s "export of religious extremism and intolerance to other countries" at a press conference announcing Saudi Arabia"s CPC designation.

In mid-2007, the Commission visited Saudi Arabia to assess the government"s progress in implementing textbook reform and other policies. However, based on that visit and subsequent research into Saudi government textbooks, including those used at the ISA, the Commission concluded that despite some improvements, these commitments, regrettably, remain largely unfulfilled.

In every official meeting during the visit to Saudi Arabia, the Commission delegation asked Saudi interlocutors for copies of textbooks. The Saudi government"s refusal to make them available during that visit or after the Commission"s return, despite repeated requests, left the Commission with continued concerns about their content and serious questions about whether they were in fact being reformed. The Commission also sought to obtain the textbooks used at the ISA. Until the Commission drew attention to the problem at a press conference in October 2007, the ISA publicly stated on its Web site that it adhered to the official Saudi government curriculum. The Commission called for the ISA to be closed under the terms of the Foreign Missions Act until the official Saudi textbooks used at the school were made available for comprehensive public examination. Soon after the Commission released its October 2007 report, the ISA dropped the language on its Web site stating that its Arabic-language and Islamic studies curriculum "is based on the Curriculum of the Saudi Ministry of Education." In the months following the Commission"s report, the Saudi government has also posted copies of the official 2007-2008 Saudi textbooks on the Internet.

Members of Congress, some of whom had also sought in vain to obtain official Saudi textbooks for review, have joined the Commission in expressing concern. In November 2007, Reps. Frank Wolf (R–VA), Steve Israel (D–NY), and Anthony Weiner (D–NY) introduced a resolution, H.Con.Res. 262, calling on the State Department to heed the Commission"s requests regarding the ISA and to create a mechanism to monitor implementation of the 2006 Saudi commitments to improving educational materials. Twelve U.S. Senators, led by Sens. John Kyl (R–AZ) and Charles Schumer (D–NY), wrote a bipartisan letter to Secretary of State Condoleezza Rice the same month, echoing the Commission"s call for closing the ISA until the official Saudi textbooks used at the school were made available for comprehensive public examination in the United States.

While neither the ISA nor the Royal Embassy of Saudi Arabia complied with the Commission"s requests to release the school"s books publicly, the Commission did obtain some Arabic–language books currently used in the twelfth grade and a random selection of texts currently used in middle and high school classes. The Commission"s review of these textbooks found that they did contain passages justifying violence toward, and even the killing of, apostates and so–called polytheists. The texts also include highly intolerant passages about non–Sunni Muslims, such as Shi"a, Ismaili, and Ahmadis, and non–Muslims, such as Jews and Baha"is. A list of the books reviewed is appended to this statement.

The ISA and Claims of Revisions

The ISA operates as an arm of the Saudi government. The ISA"s board is chaired by the Saudi ambassador to Washington, it is located on two properties, one of which is owned, the other leased, by the Saudi Embassy, and it shares the Embassy"s Internal Revenue Service employer tax number under the name of the "Royal Embassy of Saudi Arabia." It is part of a network of 19 international schools run by the government of Saudi Arabia. The ISA distributed some textbooks during a series of open houses held for selected reporters and congressional staffers after the Commission"s press conference, but it did not make available the texts with the most problematic passages–*Tawhid* (monotheism) and *Tafsir* (Koranic interpretation)–which the Commission obtained from other sources.

Last fall, after the Commission held a press conference, ISA personnel were quoted in the media as saying that they had already revised the Saudi Ministry of Education textbooks used at the school. However, the books reviewed by the Commission in the winter of 2007–2008 show evidence of truncation, omission, cutting and pasting, and the use of correction tape or fluid to cover over text–but not sufficient revision to remove all objectionable material, as evidenced by the passages cited above. They appear to be Saudi Ministry of Education textbooks, with some alterations but with identical wording in many sections of the texts.

Bilateral and International Commitments by the Saudi Government

The Saudi government is bound by more than just its 2006 confirmation of policies with the United States. The Universal Declaration of Human Rights not only guarantees religious freedom and bans discrimination and incitement to discrimination on a number of bases, including religion; it also provides specifically that education "shall promote understanding, tolerance and friendship among all nations, racial or religious groups..." The UN Declaration on the Elimination of All Forms of Intolerance and of Discrimination based on Religion or Belief also bans such discrimination, which it calls "an affront to human dignity," a "disavowal of the principles of the [UN] Charter," a violation of international human rights law, and "an obstacle to friendly and peaceful relations between nations." That Declaration, moreover, specifically provides that "[t]he child shall be protected from any form of discrimination on the ground of religion or belief. He shall be brought up in a spirit of understanding, tolerance, friendship among peoples, peace and universal brotherhood, [and] respect for freedom of religion or belief of others. . . ." The UN Convention on the Rights of the Child, to which Saudi Arabia is a party, contains similar provisions mandating non–discrimination and the teaching of tolerance in education. The UN Convention on the Elimination of All Forms of Racial Discrimination also calls on States Parties, which include Saudi Arabia, "to guarantee the right of everyone, without distinction as to race, color, or national or ethnic origin, to equality before the law" in the enjoyment of rights including "the right to freedom of thought, conscience, and religion."

Those provisions stand in stark contrast to the problematic passages that continue to appear in the ISA textbooks. It is deeply troubling that high school students at a foreign government–operated school in the United States are discussing when and under what circumstances killing an "unbeliever" would be acceptable. The U.S. government must ensure that the Saudi government thoroughly reviews and, as necessary, revises the books it has distributed globally. In both the UN Human Rights Council and UN General Assembly, Saudi Arabia has co–sponsored and supported repeated resolutions urging UN member states to "take resolute action to prohibit the dissemination . . . of racist and xenophobic ideas and material aimed at any religion or its followers that constitute incitement to racial and religious hatred, hostility or violence" and to "ensure that all public officials, including . . . educators, in the course of their official duties, respect different religions and beliefs and do not discriminate against persons on the grounds of their religion or belief." The U.S. government should insist that the Saudi government meet these commitments fully as a member in good standing of the international community.

Recommendations for the U.S. Department of State

The Commission reiterates its recommendations that the State Department should:

- make available all textbooks that it has received from the Saudi government, so that their content and compliance with international human rights standards can be assessed; and

- promptly create a formal mechanism to monitor and encourage implementation of the Saudi government"s 2006 policies as part of every meeting of the U.S.–Saudi Arabia Strategic Dialogue, and ensure that U.S. representatives to each relevant Working Group of the Strategic Dialogue, after each session, or at least every six months, report the group"s findings to Congress.

The Commission reaffirms that governments have a clear obligation to teach tolerance, not hatred. No government should be teaching children that it is justified to kill anyone on the basis of his or her religion or belief. The Commission is seriously concerned that the Saudi government is not abiding by the policies it confirmed in 2006 to promote greater religious freedom and tolerance, including by revising its school textbooks. The texts used at the ISA are only one example.

APPENDIXIslamic Saudi Academy Arabic‑Language Textbooks Reviewed by the Commission

Monotheism (Tawhid), Twelfth Grade, Administrative, Social, Natural, and Technical Sciences Track

Monotheism (Tawhid), Twelfth Grade, Sharia and Arabic Sciences Track

Interpretation (Tafsir), Twelfth Grade, Sharia and Arabic Sciences Track

Interpretation (Tafsir), Twelfth Grade, Administrative, Social, Natural, and Technical Sciences Track

Hadith and Islamic Culture, Twelfth Grade, Administrative, Social, Natural, and Technical Sciences Track

Hadith and Islamic Culture, Twelfth Grade, Sharia and Arabic Sciences Track

Jurisprudence (Fiqh), Twelfth Grade, Natural Sciences Track

Jurisprudence (Fiqh), Twelfth Grade, Sharia and Arabic Sciences Track

The History of the Kingdom of Saudi Arabia, Twelfth Grade, Natural Sciences Track

Sociology, Twelfth Grade, Sharia and Arabic Sciences Track

Studies from the Islamic World, Twelfth Grade, Administrative, Social, Natural, and Technical Sciences Track

Hadith, Seventh Grade

Hadith, Ninth Grade

Jurisprudence (Fiqh), Ninth Grade

Jurisprudence (Fiqh), Tenth Grade

Aspects of Muslim Political and Cultural History, Eleventh Grade, Administrative and Social Track, Sharia and Arabic Track

History of the Prophets, the Prophet's Biography, and the Spread of Islam, Tenth Grade

Tags: SAUDI ARABIA

www.ingramcontent.com/pod-product-compliance
Lightning Source LLC
Chambersburg PA
CBHW080857260726
48660CB00009B/3340